12/2/2011

To Adrian (a very special person)

Wishing you a very happy birthday

Love & Light

Marian & Don
  x   x

Genesis 7

GENESIS 7

L. Farra

VANTAGE PRESS
New York / Washington / Atlanta
Los Angeles / Chicago

FIRST EDITION

All rights reserved, including the right of
reproduction in whole or in part in any form.

Copyright © 1987 by L. Farra

Published by Vantage Press, Inc.
516 West 34th Street, New York, New York 10001

Manufactured in the United States of America
ISBN: 0-533-07034-1

Library of Congress Catalog Card No.: 86-90081

To Marianne, Stephen, and Russell and with special thanks to Rose, Gloria, and Peggy for their help and interest.

ACKNOWLEDGMENTS

Without the help of Gerry Sherrick, this book could not have been written. At no financial benefit to himself, he gave much of his time and energy in helping me to complete my research. This, however, is typical of him, for over the years he has helped numerous people who have sought his assistance as a medium.

Gerry has received much praise from the psychic press for his valuable work on poltergeist cases, but he is also, I would add, a highly talented poet, who has read many of his compositions on B.B.C. radio and on television programs both in England and America.

While writing this acknowledgment, my thoughts also go out to Gerry's wife, Mildred, who unfortunately passed away before I was able to complete this book. Mildred was a fine person who is sadly missed by all who knew her.

The author also wished to thank the following publishers for having generously given permission to use quotations from copyrighted works:

The History and Origins of Druidism by Lewis Spence. Reprinted by permission of Rider & Co., of the Hutchinson Publishing Group.
The Search for Lost Cities by James Wellard. Reprinted by permission of Constable Publishers.
Extracts from *Earth in Upheaval* by Immanuel Velikovsky. Copyright©1955 by Immanuel Velikovsky. Reprinted by permisson of Doubleday & Company, Inc.
Extracts from *Gateway to Oblivion* by Hugh Cochrane. Reprinted by permission of Doubleday & Company, Inc.
Pathways to the Gods by Tony Morrison. Reprinted by permission of Michael Russell (Publishing) Ltd.
Egyptian Myth and Legend, Myths of Babylonia and Assyria, Myths from Pre-Columbian America, Myths of Pre-Hellenic Europe, and *Teutonic Myth and Legend* by Donald A. Mackenzie. Reprinted by permission of Blackie and Son Limited.
Gods and Spacemen in the Ancient East by W. Raymond Drake. Reprinted by permission of the author.
Atlantis Rising by Brad Steiger. Reprinted by permission of Sphere Books Limited.
Ancient Times by James Henry Breasted. Copyright ©

1916. Used by permission of the publisher, Ginn and Company (Xerox Corporation).

Ancient Iraq by Georges Roux. Reprinted by permission of George Allen & Unwin (Publishers) Ltd.

Technology in the Ancient World by Henry Hodges. Reprinted by permission of Winant, Towers Limited.

Peru Before Pizarro by Georges Bankes. Reprinted by permission of St. Martin's Press, Inc.

The Golden Bough by J.G. Fraser. Reprinted by permission of St. Martin's Press, Inc.

Star Maps by William R. Fix. Reprinted by permission of the author.

Seth Speaks by Jane Roberts. Copyright©1972 by Jane Roberts. Reprinted by permission of the publisher, Prentice-Hall, Inc., Englewood Cliffs, New Jersey 07632.

Secrets of the Lost Races by Rene Noorbergen. Reprinted by permission of New English Library Limited.

Exploration Fawcett by Col. P.H. Fawcett. Reprinted by permission of Hutchinson Publishing Group Limited.

For an article reprinted from *The Daily Telegraph*. Reprinted by permission.

Viewpoint Aquarious and *Realty of Occult/Yoga/Meditation/Flying Saucers* by Rex Dutta. Reprinted by permission of the author.

INTRODUCTION

Thousands of years ago the most incredible happenings took place on Earth. So great was their effect that allegorical stories and related symbols became an important part of world religion. Even in today's world religious beliefs, rituals, customs, literature, film titles, place names, and commercial names unknowingly recall one of the most momentous eras in the history of man.

A few years ago I had a fascinating and incredibly accurate sitting with a clairvoyant in Bournemouth, southwest England. "You are artistic," she said, "not in painting but in writing." She then said that I had written a book and explained its theme. "It is important," she continued, "that you inform people of what you have discovered for your book tells the truth of Earth's past. At first," she explained, "it will be published in America and after that it may follow in other countries."

Genesis 7

Chapter One

The power and mystery of the paranormal has fascinated humanity throughout the centuries. Doubt and scepticism as to the survival of the soul or spirit first gave me cause to question my beliefs, so I attended the College of Psychic Studies in London, hoping that some study of the subject of spiritualism would enlighten me. After some time I came to accept that it is possible, with the help of a medium, to speak with parted loved ones, so providing comfort for thousands who believe in afterlife. I also found that the spirit guide of the circle and other spirit entities, by using the vocal cords of the medium, bespoke words of wisdom.

Several months after I first became interested in the subject, I met Gerry Sherrick, a well-known trance medium and poet, who kindly invited me to attend his circle meetings. My first visit to his home took place on the evening of the 14 September 1978. After arriving, I was ushered into a darkened room and was introduced to several people who had been waiting for me. A spare chair was then found, and after I was comfortably seated, Gerry opened the proceedings with a prayer that was followed by a few minutes of silence. While I was peering at my companions, through the darkness I suddenly became aware of a coldness in the room and, to my amazement, saw that Gerry seemed to be growing taller and that his features were changing. Very soon, he began breathing heavily and seemed to be going into a trance. Then, through him, we were greeted by the loud and distinctive voice of "White Cloud," the guide of the circle, who warmly welcomed me to the meeting. White Cloud, I later discovered had, during his physical life, been a chief of the North American Shoshone Indians.

During the next half-hour, I sat there fascinated, watching Gerry's appearance changing several times as a series of spirit entities entered his body and spoke to my companions and to me. At the end of the session, when he came out of trance, I had many questions to ask, and we discussed some of the many aspects of spiritualism. There then followed a demonstration of clairvoyance, and one of the mediums told me that I would be giving talks on the subject and would be involved in writing. This, however, I found hard to accept, for nothing was further from my mind at the time.

At another circle meeting held at the Sherricks' home on 1 August 1979, one of the mediums present informed me that she felt strongly impressed to tell me that I should visit a certain North London second-hand–goods shop. I listened attentively as she told me the name of the street and area that, although fairly well known to me, left me none the wiser. Three days later, hoping to satisfy my curiosity and having a couple of hours to spare, I set off for North London. It was a dismal day, raining heavily when I arrived, so I parked my car and briskly walked past several houses and a small parade of uninteresting shops until eventually I found myself standing outside a dilapidated wooden building filled with dusty, old furniture and ornaments. After looking in from the safety of the doorway, I cautiously ventured inside, hoping that the proprietor would not offer assistance for, after all, I could hardly tell him the purpose of my visit.

Fortunately, within a few moments, I noticed a shelf, crowded with old books, tucked away behind a large table in the far corner; and so, now having an excuse for being there, I made my way between the lines of stacked furniture to take a closer look. Very soon my eyes were drawn to a large, dusty volume that somehow seemed to be begging for my attention. I glanced through the contents and, finding them of interest, paid the proprietor and left with my purchase.

M. Oldfield Howey's *The Horse in Myth and Magic* was my first "prompted" purchase. In it, the author relates several variations of the Legend of the Seven Sleepers and says that Hindus believed that "seven horses" draw the golden chariot of the sun.[1]

Although of general interest, the book had no special significance until three weeks later. Gerry Sherrick and I had been having a discussion about UFOs and he said that the "wheel within a wheel," reputed to have been seen by Ezekiel (Ezek. 1:16), sounded remarkably like one of those mysterious objects that occasionally flash through our skies. With my curiosity once again aroused, I decided to read through the Bible to see whether any of the other "miracles" warranted a nonreligious interpretation. Starting with the Book of Genesis, I made my way through the well-known biblical stories and, in so doing, was fascinated to find that in most of these the number seven was given prominence.

I decided to extend my study to other religions and was amazed to discover that the mystical seven is featured not only in Judaism but also in Hinduism, Buddhism, Islam, and many other religions.

At this stage, I was unable to determine the reason for this custom. In fact, until I drew attention to it, people to whom I spoke seemed unaware of the widespread fascination with this number. The mystery, however, was short-lived, for a most sensational revelation was awaiting me.

On the evening of 25 August 1979, Gerry became aware that, standing near the window in the lounge of his home, there appeared to be the shadowy outline of an American Indian. He barely had time to alert his family, when the entity moved swiftly across the room and entered his body. Introducing himself to Gerry's wife and sons as Quatal, he told them that, when on the earth plane, he was leader of his tribe in the country now known as Mexico. He then related how, one day, some of his people had rushed to his home to tell him that huge circular birds were in the sky. By the time he went to investigate, however, the strange birds had landed. For a while nothing happened; then, to the astonishment of the Indians, from the birds came tall white men who made contact with them and accompanied them back to their camp. Quatal gave no further details other than to explain that the disc he wore round his neck was a replica of the craft of the white men, made by craftsmen of his tribe. Then, as suddenly as he had come, Quatal departed, having told the Sherricks that he would return another time and tell them more.

When Gerry came out of trance, his family told him of Quatal's incredible disclosures. On the following day, the happenings were related to me. Gerry was extremely excited over this strange, unexpected visitation and said he would arrange a meeting of his circle to try to contact this "Indian spirit-guide."

A meeting was arranged for the evening of 30 August 1979. Present were the Sherricks, two mediums, myself, and my wife, Marianne. The seance was now ready to begin. Apprehensively, we sat in the darkened room spread out in a circle. At Gerry's request we closed our eyes and sent thoughts to Quatal, asking that he should appear. We did not have long to wait, for suddenly, there was a sharp drop in the room's temperature and, as if in answer to my unasked question, Gerry announced Quatal's anxiously awaited arrival.

One of the mediums excitedly exclaimed that she could see Quatal whom she described as having long, fine, silvery hair. As my wife and I are not clairvoyant, it was explained to us that the Indian wore a band across his forehead, animal skins over his shoulders, and a peculiar ring on one of his fingers.

A few minutes later, Gerry's features and stature began to change, and we realized Quatal had entered his body. "My name," said our visitor, "is Quatal, and when I was on your earth plane I lived in that part of the world you now call the Americas, at the time when strange men came down from the heavens to visit earth. These men were much different to my people; they were taller, light of skin; some were gifted with a third eye for clairvoyant vision. After they emerged from their craft, much heat came from them, and when some of my people went too close their skins became affected. They brought with them special tools for cutting and machines that caused heavy objects to levitate from the ground. While they were with us, they taught us many new things, and gave me a strange ring which emitted a ray." Quatal then departed and once again promised to return.

A couple of weeks later he came to Gerry and told him that "seven craft" had visited Mexico and in each of these were seven men. The jigsaw puzzle was now beginning to make sense.

On the following day, the Sherrick family had a visit from another spirit-guide who was tall of stature, white-haired and who was dresssed in a long white robe. A gold chain hung from his neck, and he carried a long crystal staff that continually changed color.

For many months, this spirit entity took keen interest in the progression of my book and, sometimes, while I was in Gerry's company, he too would be there. On occasions he would give advice through Gerry.

On one of my visits to Gerry, he and I discussed the third psychic eye of the spacemen who, for convenience and because the name was used by some spiritual informants, I shall call the "Travelers." Gerry said he felt it resembled an eye but that it was more to one side of the forehead and did not seem part of the physical body.

A few days later, Gerry was visited by Quatal, who told him that "the Travelers" used diamonds in the propulsion systems of their craft. He also said that I should study the symbols of the ancient Egyptian gods and research into *The Lost Continent of Atlantis*.

On 4 October 1979, Gerry told me that, clairvoyantly, he had seen craft descending from the sky attached to supports resembling parachutes. After they had landed, men emerged.

On 20 November 1979, I went to a meeting of the Sherricks' circle. Gerry went into trance and we had the pleasure of being spoken to by Quatal, who had, once again, taken over his body:

"When I last spoke to you, I told of strange men from the heavens who visited my people. Unlike us, they had no need to speak, for they could communicate direct with the mind. They carried unusual staffs that had many uses and while with us showed us how to use diamonds for cutting and taught us many other things. They told us that they came from beyond the time barrier and that before leaving they would give us a machine that could be used to contact them. So that man could advance from his present state, the seeds from the Travelers were sown in the wombs of our daughters, in order that great leaders would be born."

A meeting was addressed by Quatal on 12 December 1979, in the home of the Sherrick family, and for the first time it was taped. On this occasion, Quatal had the following to say:

"Greetings to you, my friends; greetings, my sisters and my brothers. I am pleased once more to be allowed to speak through the voice of the instrument. My name is Quatal and I used the medium's body when I last visited you. There are many things that you wish to know, but there are only certain things that I am allowed to tell you. When I lived on your earth plane, I was not a clever man in your ways, but I was a clever man in the ways of my people. When I spoke with you last time, I told you of the coming of seven stars. I told you how, from the seven stars, men came, and how we were not allowed to go near to them; but, after a period of time, they emerged from the outer covering, and they showed us and taught us many things.

"They told us that their leader would not appear to us but that, in time, one of us would be chosen to enter into one of their stars to speak with their Lord, their leader.

"When we ate our food, they did not eat with us. We ate the flesh of the animal, but they ate little colored pebbles taken from their little box. They had blue pebbles, green pebbles, and we were amazed that this was their food. They did not drink of our water, nor did they partake of our wines. They just used . . . how I say? . . . They just used . . . I cannot explain in your language, but they just used their own water that they carried in containers. But their only food was the little round blue pebbles and green pebbles, but never the food that we offered them.

"After many moons I, Quatal, was chosen to enter

into one of their stars, but first my body had to be cleansed. This they did by shining lights over my body. Then, they dressed me in a robe of white with white sandals on my feet, and they led me into their star, and I was very much afraid. Inside the star were many colored lights, and they took me into a room, but I was afraid because the doors of the room slid open by themselves. They told me they would leave me there. They sat me down and told me not to be afraid. But I was afraid, because I am only an ignorant man and did not understand the way of these travelers. And then I felt very happy and I smelt many beautiful fragrances and I looked in front of me and there was a cabinet with a beautiful curtain in front of the cabinet. And I was told to close my eyes.

"Then I heard the voice of their Lord, who spoke to me, telling me that they came from far out in space. He told me that they would teach my people many things, and all that we were told and shown must be in the ways of peace and love.

"He asked me if there were any questions that I wished to ask him. And I asked him, 'What name are you called, Master?' And he said, 'I am called Lord.' And I said, 'But I am also called Lord by my people.' And he said, 'My name is Goda.' And he said, 'I am called Lord Goda.'

"He told me to stretch out my hand, but I must not look, I must keep my eyes closed. And I stretched out my hands. He placed in my hands a staff of light. And he said to me, 'Lord Goda says that if I am in need, the staff will be of assistance to me to contact Lord Goda.'

"And then I went to sleep, and when I opened my eyes again, I was outside of the star. And I looked at what Lord Goda had given me and it was a staff of shining light. And I was told by one of the men from the star that this staff had power of healing, and that if there came a time when my people were in need of water, the staff, being knocked against the rock, would produce water. He told me that if my people were ever in need, to find gold or diamonds from the earth, the staff would lead me to them. The staff would stop on the position where I needed to find what I was seeking.

"He told me that his name on his earth was Mikal. He told me that his companion was called Gabriel and that they would visit us again. He said they were going to visit other parts of the earth where they would train and show other people. But he told me to remember the words of Lord Goda: to use the weapons in peace. He said to remember to be clean in thought, to be clean in body, and to remember their visit. He said that some of the Travelers who had come with him had mingled with my women and that they would give forth children. But these children would not look the same as my tribe. They would be high in statute (stature). They would have an eye in the center of their heads. But I must remember to treat them with reverence and love.

"Then the stars departed and they were seen no more. We learned, many moons later, that there had been much evil, that those in other parts of the world . . . had not used the instruments that the Travelers left for the purposes of peace. They had abused the teachings of Lord Goda, and Lord Goda had grown wild with anger and sent forth his bolts from heaven."

With Quatal's departure, there was a break of a couple of minutes, during which Gerry's appearance once again changed. This time, we were addressed by a more cultured, yet rather distressed personality:

"I, I am the High Priest. I am the High Priest of Atlantai. I told my people, 'Do not use these weapons to destroy.' I told my people, 'Do not seek for gold but seek to heal the sick.' I told my people to use the instruments that Lord Goda gave us, to make peace on Earth, but that they were filled with jealousy and their minds were filled with evil. But, when the Lord Goda departed in the spirit, he left behind destruction."

On 4 March 1981, I was invited to the Sherrick family's home with a friend who, though a nonbeliever, was interested in learning about spiritualism. Gerry spent some time describing his work as a medium and told of some of the fascinating poltergeist cases in which he had been involved. Later in the evening, he went into trance and, once again, his features changed, and he appeared to grow taller.

We found ourselves in the company of an "Indian" who told how, during his physical life, he had lived in the cold lands of North America. He said that he had been an astrologer and that it was customary for him to stay out at night and study the stars. Wild animals did not worry him, for he did not trouble them.

He went on to tell how, one night, he had dressed in warm furs, put on snowshoes, and went out to observe the heavens. After traveling for an hour or so he had laid down, covered himself over, and soon was asleep. He awoke to find what appeared to be a brightly lit, colored bird hovering above him and, to his amazement, bright rays shone down, causing the snow to melt. Standing before him, appeared a tall man clad in a long white robe. Speaking directly with his mind, the latter introduced himself as Mikal and explained that he had come from beyond the time barrier.

"Then," said our informant, "he asked me to hold out my hands; I felt a heat on them and found I was holding a large red stone resembling a diamond. He told me this could be cut into pieces and used as tools. He said he would visit my people and teach many things, but he warned that much trouble would be coming to our country in the future."

On 15 September 1979, Gerry had another visit from Quatal, who told him that the Travelers emerged from their craft wearing close-fitting, gold-colored garments and, that this had so astounded the Indians, they were completely convinced that their visitors had arrived "from the sun." Quatal added that the "starmen" had later removed these garments and appeared to the Indians dressed in long white robes.

While these various spiritual communications were being received, and, indeed, continuously since that time, I have researched for supporting evidence, part of which I now lay before you.

In the traditions of the Torajas of Indonesia, it is said that, long ago, "seven mysterious objects" appeared after which men were "created in gold."

In ancient Israel, in the Yom Kippur service at the temple in Jerusalem, the high priest was bathed and then dressed in a "golden" garment. During the service, he tended seven-stemmed candlesticks and changed into a white robe. Shortly, we shall see these candlesticks represent the "seven heavens."

In *The Book of the Secrets of Enoch*, written in Egypt some eighteen to nineteen hundred years ago, it says that when Enoch visited the "seventh heaven" he saw Michael who was instructed by the Lord "to take away his clothing and present him with the garment of the Lord." This, according to the Jewish Midrash, was a long white robe.

Not without significance in some Orthodox Jewish weddings, the bridegroom, dressed in a long white robe, is "circled" seven times by the bride, her mother, and his mother, while the ancient Egyptians taught how the gods dressed in long white robes and white sandals.

Various scholars have wondered why the Central American Maya Indians and the ancient Egyptians, both clean-shaven, should have depicted their gods with beards. Cabalists say that one of the reasons why Jewish men should grow beards is that, by doing so, they preserve their likeness to God. In other words, according to Jewish sources, the Lord was a bearded man who wore a long white robe.

Michael (who is like unto God), the emissary of the Lord and greatest of all angels to Jews, Moslems, and Christians, is said by the Talmud to be chief of "seven spirits" and "prince of waters." Blavatsky says that the latter is another name for the "great deep"—the primordial waters of space.[2]

Throughout the Americas, the Indians tell of a white-robed, white-bearded, white god who once came to earth, taught their ancestors agriculture and civilization, and preached brotherly love. The tribes that he is said to have visited gave him a variety of names. The most interesting of these is found among the Nothern American Algonquin Indians, who tell how, long ago, the great spirit sent to earth "Michabo" (The Great White One), who helped resettle the survivors of the flood.

In Colombia, South America, the Muscans have traditions of a "golden man" and of a civilizing white god called "Bochica," who had a flowing white beard, wore a long white robe and carried a golden staff. After staying with the Muscans for some time, Bochica is said to have returned to the heavens and was seen no more.

In Mexico, the claimed former homeland of Quatal, it is said that in the distant past a "winged ship" appeared and from it emerged a tall, white-bearded man. This man, one of seven gods, wore a long white robe, a golden helmet, and carried a long staff. He was known to the Central American Indians as Quetzalcoatl, Gucumatz, and Kukulcan, and is said to have taught the Indians agriculture, astronomy, and medicine. The Indians say that before he returned to the heavens, he promised that in the future white-bearded men like himself would come to the country. Thus, when the small, Spanish army arrived at Tonochlitan, the Aztec capital, no resistance was offered to them, for the Indians mistakenly thought that the white gods had returned. Quatal said that when the Travelers came to his country, one strange characteristic his people were amazed to see was their food, which consisted of "green and blue pebbles." When the Spanish army arrived in Mexico, the Indians were puzzled to find that the white gods ate food similar to theirs. The Spanish, in turn, were equally surprised to find the Indians believed that gems such as jade and emerald gave nourishment and protection and that green stones were used by them as symbols of authority. When the Spanish queried the importance of these stones, they were told that when the great white god, Quetzalcoatl, first came to Mexico, he had such stones with him and, since then, they had been revered by the Indians.

Twelve thousand five hundred feet above sea level, not far from the shore of Lake Titicaca in the Andes, are the remains of the mysterious, ancient city of Tiahuanaco. When the Spanish first arrived at the then-deserted city, they discovered the statue of a bearded man. Other statues of bearded men have been found in Ecuador, Colombia, El Salvador, Guatemala, and Mexico, while in the Mayan Lolton Cave complex, there has been found a nine-foot statue of a "winged bearded man."[3]

When Hernando de Soto arrived in Peru, the Inca ruler Hauscar told him of a prophecy passed to him by his father that said one day "divine white men" would come to earth from the sun and rule over the Incas. This tradition has obvious connections with a Peruvian legend that tells how, thousands of years ago, "tall white men" descended to earth from the sun and, after helping to civilize them, destroyed an evil race with a devastating flood. After rescuing some of the survivors, the white men departed and were seen no more.

The Peruvians called the leader of these "sun men" Viracocha and described him as an elderly, bearded white man who carried a staff and was first seen after a "brilliant sun" rose from one of the islands of Lake Titacaca. The Incas, who placed him in the highest of their seven levels of gods, say that he traveled through the highlands, working miracles and making water flow from the rocks. Everywhere he went he preached brotherly love. The Indians revered him as the creator and set up numerous statues in his likeness. They also said that Tiahuanaco's statues date to his time.

On the evening of 3 July 1980, while I and two friends were spending a social evening with Gerry and his family, Gerry suddenly announced that a spirit entity was with us and was indicating that he wished to talk to us. A few minutes later, Gerry's appearance began changing, and he entered into a state of trance.

Very soon, we saw standing before us what seemed to be a small Oriental man. After introducing himself, our visitor explained that, during his physical life, he had been a Tibetan monk. Knowledge of the Travelers' visit, he said, had been widespread throughout the ancient east, and his own distant ancestors had met them when they visited Tibet. The Tibetan monks, he added, still had a considerable amount of evidence of that visit and, although much had been destroyed by the British and Chinese when they entered the country, they still kept some hidden away in secret places.

Several months after this revelation, I discovered that, when members of a Soviet expedition visited Tibet in 1952, they were shown some ancient documents that told of a time when the earth was visited by men from another part of the universe. I also noted that Tibetan tradition claims that mankind's spiritual teachers were the "seven divine Lhas," who must surely be the "seven kings" said in Tibet to have arrived from the stars. (Presumably, they came in the "seven heavenly thrones" referred to in Tibetan writings.)

In Japan, "seven gods" are said to have arrived in a boat. One of these, Fukurokuya, is shown as an elderly, white-bearded, long-robed man carrying a staff.

In the Gobi Desert, say Chinese sources, there once was a sea surrounding an island on which lived fair-haired men who came to earth from the stars. This island is also referred to by the Bramins of India, who tell of "seven solar angels," the Kumaras, who arrived there in the mists of time.

"On the South Pacific Island of Ponape," writes Rene Noorbergen, "the natives tell of learned men, with lighter skins than their own, who came from the West before the European explorers arrived. These former light-skinned men came in shining boats which flew above the sea."[4]

On Easter Island in the Pacific, sacred writings tell of seven explorers discovering the island.

Two of the seven traditional leaders* of the Central American Quiche Mayan Indians were Mahucutah and Balam Agab (note the similarity to the names Mikal and Gabriel; *balam*, as a matter of interest, means jaguar).

---

*Four men and three women.

Babylonians told of "seven wise beings"; stories coming from Borneo tell of seven friendly gods and "seven suns." Ancient Assyrians had traditions of seven gods in "fiery spheres." People in Northern India worshiped "Sapta Mata" (the seven mothers), depicted in the form of seven domes.

Quatal asserted that each of the seven craft carried seven men. Writings in the Hindu mythological poem, "Vaya Purana" refer to the "seven and seven rishis." Blavatsky tells of rishis who have become informing souls of the seven stars. "Seven times seven," she adds, "is a transparent allegory to the Forty-nine Manus," (divine beings from another plane).[5] Similarly, the Celts claimed that long ago there came to Ireland forty-nine divine beings called Parthalon's people, who arrived from the "other world," obtained seven lakes and, after destroying an evil race, departed.

The Book of the Secrets of Enoch discloses that Enoch was taken to a place where he saw "seven groups of angels" studying the movements of the stars. Above the angels were the archangels—the divine teachers. The archangels are seven in number, two of whom are Michael and Gabriel.

Quatal also reported that the leader of the Travelers was called Goda or Godai. The Aleutian islanders call their supreme diety "Agudar," the ancient Peruvians knew the supreme god as "Ataguja," while the ancient Gallu people in Europe claimed that their ancestors once lived in a land to the west. It was here they were civilized by Hu Gadarn, who led them to their new homelands. The Tartars speak of a supreme deity "Kutai" and of "seven kutais" who live in a tent in the sky.

Although Quatal did not mention a possible parent craft, there is much in religion and mythology to suggest there was one. Phoenician mythology tells how Aleyin traveled through the skies with seven others.[6] The Greeks allude to Atlas hovering above while his seven daughters sped through the skies, and in India it is said that Krishna had a "favorite wife" and seven secondary ones who similarly traveled at great speed. A Teutonic legend explains how the great god Thor witnessed the descent of a huge kettle and in its wake seven smaller ones. Ancient Egyptians believed in a "heavenly herd," consisting of a bull and seven cows. The secret society of Rosicrucians have as an emblem a pelican feeding its seven offspring. In Mexico are writings known as "Chilam Balam of Chumayel." These cite that the Almighty created the "Great Stone of Grace," from which emerged "seven smaller stones." West African Dogon acknowledge "eight ancestors," the eighth of whom was older than the other seven. This eighth ancestor rose "into the heavens," closely followed by the other seven.

In the Book of Genesis, in the Bible, it is said that Enoch "walked with God." *The Book of Enoch*, however, suggests that it was not in fact God whom he saw: "And I raised mine eyes again to heaven and I saw a vision and behold there came forth from the heaven, beings who were like white men and four went forth from that place and three with them."[7]

The New Testament, Rev. 4:1–2, tells of an encounter which would appear to have associations with the seven white men mentioned by Enoch: "After this I looked and behold, a door was opened in heaven and the first voice which I heard was as it were of a trumpet talking with me which said come hither and I will show things which must be hereafter."

This reference to a "speaking trumpet" is interesting, bearing in mind Quatal's experience in one of the "seven stars." "And immediately, I was in the Spirit," continues

John, "and behold a throne was set in heaven, and one sat on the throne in sight like an emerald. And around the throne were four and twenty seats; and upon the seats I saw four and twenty elders sitting, clothed in white rainment; and they had on their heads crowns of gold.

"Out of the throne," said John, "proceedeth lightnings and thunderings and voices. And there were seven lamps of fire burning before the throne, which are the seven spirits of God."

Here it can be seen that these seven fiery spirits were within a large, enclosed space known as heaven or "the spirit."

At the time "of the Jerusalem temple" during the Yom Kippur service, a bull was slaughtered, and some of its blood was taken to the Holy of Holies. There it was sprinkled by the high priest who counted "one above" and "seven below."[8] The deep significance behind this ritual was suggested by the third-century Babylonian rabbi Aha Ben Jacob, who said that surmounting the seven heavens is an eighth.

North American Ojibway Indian sources relate that a thunderbird once caused terrible destruction on earth. Ojibway legend tells of "White Beaver," one of seven Indian brothers, who was married to one of seven thunderbird's sisters.[9] Since the "seven flying sisters" had two parents, it would appear that their mother had a consort.

In precommunist Peking, it was customary for the emperor to pray in a building known as the Temple of Heaven. On the highest of the three levels were nine concentric circles symbolising the nine heavens. Nine worlds appear in Scandinavian traditions. In Central American, the Maya built nine-tiered structures reflecting the nine levels or nine heavenly residences linked with the nine lords of the night.

Ancient Egyptian texts show nine gods standing on a flight of nine steps on the summit of which sits the bearded, white-robed, staff-carrying, civilizing god known to the Egyptians as Osiris. Of similar description was the Mayan civilizing god Kukulcan to whom a nine-tiered step pyramid was dedicated at Chichen Itza in Yucatan, Mexico.

Hermetic teachings tell of a ninth heaven above the eighth, which in turn surmounts the other seven. The North American Hopi Indians believe that the Supreme Creator is in the ninth world. His nephew is in the eighth. Japanese tradition adds that "before the seven generations of gods, two other gods arrived but later disappeared."

Chapter Two

In January, 1980, a business associate told me of an occult bookshop that was well worth visiting. When I mentioned this to Gerry, he too advised me to go for I would discover there a book which would be of special interest. While browsing through books on mysticism, religion, astrology, and many occult subjects I noticed H.P. Blavatsky's *The Secret Doctrine*, which makes many revealing comments on the mystical seven and shows that deep significance was given to it in the ancient world.

"Seven, by its occult virtues," quotes Blavatsky from Hippocrates, "tended to the accomplishment of all things, to be the dispenser of life and fountain of all its changes."[10]

The number seven, designated by the Egyptians as "The symbol of Eternal Life," featured prominently in every major world religion. The Israelites claimed that on the seventh day the Lord rested, hence the seven-day week, the seventh day (the Sabbath) being the most holy. The septenary is stressed throughout the Bible in the stories of Lamech, Jacob, Samson, Job, Solomon, Ruth, Moses, Esther, and others, and extensively, as we shall see, in that of Noah.

So enthralled were the ancient people with the number seven, it was introduced in religious rituals covering every important aspect of life and is still in evidence in this present age, especially among Jews, Moslems, Hindus, and Buddhists. Some of the most revealing of these can now be considered.

The *Tefillen* (phylacteries), worn by Jewish males in their morning service, consists of two black boxes attached to leather straps, one of which is placed on the forehead between the eyes and the other on the left arm with its strap wound round seven times. In a burial custom of some Sephardic Jews, the grave is circled seven times, while in the days of the temple in Jerusalem, on the seventh day of the festival of Succoth (Tabernacles), the priests circled the ark an equivalent number of times.

The theme is repeated in the Bible, wherein the story of the capture of Jericho, seven priests with seven trumpets circled the city for seven days; on the seventh they circled it seven times.

Islam requires devout pilgrims to Mecca to circle the holy Caaba stone seven times. In North Africa, people would circle a fire seven times to guard against evil, and in ancient Egypt it was customary for priests to walk seven times around a temple carrying a statue of the god Aion.

English folklore has us believe that if certain sites were circled seven times the devil would appear. In Sri Lanka, a tooth claimed to be that of Buddha is kept in the seventh of seven concentric caskets. In a tomb in Yemen, a woman from an earlier age was found buried with seven rows of pearls around her neck, seven bracelets on her wrists, and seven ankle rings round her feet. It is customary at a Burmese birth for cotton to be wound in seven circles round the baby's wrist, ankle, and neck, and for the cradle to be rocked seven times.

Temples of the mystery religions were sometimes built in the form of seven linked circles. At a London exhibition of North American Indian art, there was Caddoan Indian pottery decorated with seven concentric circles. This same pattern was used by the Etruscans and is found in ancient rock drawings in places as far apart as Europe and the Americas. In the funeral ceremony held for Burmese Buddhist monks, the body is laid in a wooden coffin, enclosed within a golden shell, and placed on a seven-tiered funeral pyre said to symbolize Mount Meru, the "home of the gods," which is said to be circled by seven rivers.

For several thousand years, the number seven has been widely associated with spiritual evolvement. The Central American Mayan Indians used the same word to signify seven and the ultimate, and their initiates passed through a seven-staged ritual. Buddhists acknowledge a physical plane surmounted by six spiritual levels, and, similarly, the North American Ojibway Indians claim that above the earth are the six layers of heaven, in the highest of which is the great spirit.

In Jewish burials, in Talmudic times, it was customary to make seven steps and this is still observed among some. Seven steps are claimed to have been taken by Buddha on the day of his birth and are taken by the bride and bridegroom in a Hindu marriage ceremony.

In the children's game of hopscotch, a stone symbolizing the soul is passed through seven stages. In Mahayanan Buddhism, the Bodivisattvas (heavenly beings) are said to achieve the condition of a Buddha when they reach the seventh level. Similarly, spiritualists claim that the spirit passes through seven spheres in the course of its evolvement; while in Mithraism, it was believed that the soul traveled through seven spheres in a descent at birth and then rose through them in order to achieve perfection. There were also, in Mithraism, seven grades of initiate who took seven steps; and, in Moslem Sufism, Ibn Arabi is said to have "risen through seven spheres of self."

Jewish man at prayer wearing the tephillen. Photo courtesy of Stephen Farra, from a drawing by H. Meredith.

Egyptian Papyrus Ani. Anhai's journey to heaven in a boat with seven steps. Courtesy of the British Museum.

The Ancient Egyptians believed that on its journey to god, the spirit passed through seven halls or mansions. In the Egyptian *Book of the Dead*, Anhai, a priestess of the twentieth dynasty, is pictured approaching the gods in heaven after her arrival in a vessel from whose deck rose a flight of seven steps.

In a Mochican Indian pottery painting discovered in Peru, the body of a huge serpent supports a four-tiered pyramid at the head of which sits a god or leader. In front of him is the head and upper part of the body of a second snake that follows the upward slope of the pyramid forming a base for a flight of seven steps. Approaching this stairway are two naked men carrying an important dignitary, and others are ascending.

Although not a standard synagogue feature, in an East London synagogue, seven steps lead to the ark. Jewish writings claim that when the "Messiah" comes, "golden thrones" will descend from the heavens and it will be possible to approach them by mounting seven steps.

Although the origins of Freemasonry are obscure, it can be seen that some of its symbolism and concepts bear a remarkable similarity to those of the religions of the ancient world. In Freemasonry, seven steps are taken, seven members constitute a perfect lodge, and seven masons are represented by seven stars. One of the symbols of Freemasonry is a ladder reaching to the heavens, surmounted by a seven-pointed star.

It would indeed be surprising if the mystical seven so ingrained in religious tradition were not also reflected in important buildings. We find in ancient Persia and Rome initiates used seven-stepped pyramids in the rites of Mithras. In Peru, an important pyramid with seven steps built by the Mochican Indians. In ancient Babylonia, the earliest pyramids or temples were constructed on seven levels, as are most of the important pagodas in the Far East. Seven levels were also built into several of the earliest pyramids in Egypt.

At Mamallapuram in India, the Hindus built a group of pagodas known as the "Seven Pagodas" on the roofs of which are domes called *vimanas* (in the Sanskrit language, vimanas are flying machines). The ancient Armenians had a group of seven temples dedicated to their seven most-important gods. The Maya built a group of seven temples at Tikal in Guatemala, and when excavations were carried out in 1962, there was discovered in a tomb beneath the Temple of the Great Jaguar a bone inscribed with the drawing of "seven gods in a boat."

Chapter Three

One of my friends told me that she was going to Israel, and so I took the opportunity of asking her to keep an eye open for books on Jewish religious customs. On her return to England a few weeks later, she brought me back a beautifully illustrated book on Jewish ceremonial art. In this was a photograph of the seven-stemmed Jewish candlestick (the Menorah), which, together with the author's explanation, decided my next line of investigation.[11]

The Menorah, one of the earliest known of Jewish symbols, was used as a form of religious decoration in many ancient synagogues. In the early part of the present era, it was borrowed by the Christians, who used it in their Easter ceremonies and, in later days, models of it were placed in various cathedrals such as Rheims, Paderborn, and Mollen. It is also referred to in the Book of Revelation in the New Testament where, in chapter 1, verse 12, it is connected with a man of "most unusual appearance":

And I turned to see the voice that spake to me. . . . And in the midst of the seven candlesticks one like unto the Son of man, clothed with a garment down to the foot, and girt about the paps with a golden girdle. His head and his hairs were white like wool, as white as snow; and his eyes were as a flame of fire.

The Jews and early Christians, however, were not alone in associating the number seven with fire. In a midsummer fire festival in North Africa, for example, it was customary to jump "seven times" over a fire. In a ritual of the Koragas of South Canara in India, grass is placed against seven specially constructed huts and set alight, while in Belgium, the north of France and parts of Germany, in a Lenten bonfire custom, it was said that seven bonfires should be seen to safeguard a village from fire.

According to the Hindus, Agni, the god of fire—like the Jewish menorah—has seven arms and, just as a seven-stemmed candlestick stood in Herod's temple in Jerusalem, so in Mithraic temples seven fires were kept burning before the altar of Mithra. The North American Sioux Indians identify seven with their seven campfire circles. Jewish tradition says that the seven-stemmed candlestick symbolizes the "seven heavens." These seven candlesticks, explains the book of Zechariah, "they are the eyes of the Lord, which run to and fro through the whole earth." (Zec. 4:10).

In Assyro-Babylonian mythology, the goddess Ishtar traveled in a chariot drawn by seven horses, and flying quadrupeds of a similar type appear in the well-known biblical story of Elijah: "Behold, there appeared a chariot of fire, and parted them both asunder; and Elijah went up by a whirlwind into heaven." (2 Kings 2:2).

A South American Amazonian legend tells of a wondrous person called Elipas who traveled on the back of a snake and healed the sick with his magical powers. After a while, the local rulers became angered with his miracles and, in order to escape their evil clutches, he caused his serpent to send down fire to destroy their land. After lecturing the survivors, Elipas mounted his fiery serpent and disappeared into the heavens.

Similarly, in the story of Elijah, prior to his departure into the skies, heavenly fire was sent down, destroying those attempting to arrest him; and, in a Peruvian myth, we are told that, before departing from earth, the white-bearded god Viracocha was oppressed by an evil people who were destroyed when he called down fire from the heavens.

Snake worship, linked with the mystical seven, has prevailed throughout the ages in all parts of the world. In ancient Egypt, there were legends of a giant seven-headed serpent called "Apep" (The Great Worm) and of seven serpents (The Ureaus), one of whom attacked the enemies of God. In his writings in the *Lost Pacific Continent of Mu*, James Churchward decoded an ancient creation story that tells of the journey through space of the seven-headed serpent and of its eggs hatching in the sea.[12] Hindus claim that the god Vishnu traveled through space in a deep sleep on the back of a seven-headed serpent called "Sesha." Among the ruins of the city of Anuradhapura in Sri Lanka and at the ancient temple of Angkor Thom in Cambodia, one can find many statues of snakes of such description.

El Tajin, in the state of Veracruz in southeast Mexico, is believed to have been built by the Haustecs, a people related to the Maya. In the center of this large complex stands the seven-tiered Temple of the Niches, which seems to have featured prominently in the religious life of the people who lived in the area. On the summit of this temple, archaeologists have discovered several inscribed tablets, and one of these shows a decapitated man from whose shoulders rise seven serpents. The tablet is suggested to have been connected with the ritual ball game of the Maya, Aztecs, and other Central American Indians in which the ball is said to represent the "star of the sun god" on its journey through the heavens. The game is suggested to be connected with the descent to earth of god-seven.[13]

While I was traveling through Mexico, I visited Uxmal, in the Yucatan, to discover that on one of its temples is depicted seven rattlesnakes. I also went to the Mayan and later Toltec complex of Chichen Itza, and there on a wall in the main ballcourt, I saw a frieze that showed seven men said to represent the team. From the shoulders of one of the men (who was decapitated) rose seven serpents. While I was examining this picture, I listened to the guide's suggestion as to how the game appears to have been played. When he had finished, the courier accompanying my party, who had lived in Spain for many years, said that the game seemed similar to the Basque ball game. "That is interesting," I exclaimed, "for there are seven serpents in this picture, and the seven-headed serpent was of importance to the Basques." The Basques, by coincidence (?), are divided into seven regional groupings.

The language of the Basques bears no relationship to any other European language, although it is said to resemble some spoken in the Americas. Can it be coincidental that American psychic Edgar Cayce claimed that some Atlantean refugees fled to the area around the Pyrenees?[14]

At the far end of Chichen Itza's main ballcourt is a small temple known as the Temple of the Bearded Man. This is said to be named after a relief on one of its walls of an elderly bearded man believed to be the white god Kukulcan. Near the ballcourt is another building, called Kukulcan's Chapel, in which the god is depicted closely attended by priests carrying bags of rattlesnakes and being approached by another priest who carries a bowl from which protrude the heads of seven rattlesnakes.

In the late summer of 1979, a business acquaintance sent me a postcard from Mexico bearing a picture of Palenque's Temple of the Inscriptions. My attention having been drawn to this interesting building, I subsequently discovered that when archaeologists were investigating it they found that beneath its nine levels the Maya had constructed an impressive tomb for Pacal, a great ruler of the city. On a slab covering the tomb is a drawing of the sacred ceiba tree, which in Mayan tradition is said to reach from earth to the heavens. Pacal also appears in the picture, and he is shown looking up to the top of the tree on which, with a "piece of green jade" in its mouth, stands the Quetzal bird symbolizing the white-bearded god who once visited earth.

Near the Temple of the Inscriptions is the Temple of the Cross, which has an altar bearing a depiction of the goddess Chicomecohuatl (seven serpent); and on a wall of another building, known as The Palace, seven heads greet the visitors together with a frieze of the "white god."

Blavatsky, in referring to the mystical seven, states that; "It frequently occurs in the Popul Vuh. We find it besides in the seven families, said by Sahuagun and Clavigers to have accompanied the mystical person Votan, the reputed founder of the great city of Nachan, identified by some with Palenque."[15]

Votan was the Quiche version of Quetzalcoatl, and it is relevant that he led seven families. Quetzalcoatl was often depicted looking out from the mouth of a snake and was said to travel within a "shining serpent."

In the ancient world, the serpent symbol was often accompanied by a disc. In ancient Egypt, it was said that Horus took the form of a winged disc when he attacked the enemies of Ra. Isis, the mother of Horus, who was sometimes depicted with both wings and a disc, was claimed to be the wife of the world-traveling, peace-preaching god Osiris.

Says Blavatsky:

31

The Egyptian god Osiris. Courtesy of the British Museum. Photo by Stephen Farra.

Coming from the primordial water with the uraeus, which is the serpent emblem of Cosmic fire, and himself the seventh over the six primary gods issued from Father-Mother, Nou and Nout (the sky), who can Osiris be but the chief Prajapati or the chief Sephiroth? The solar and cosmic god Amshaspend-Ormaz stood in the same position as the archangel "whose name was secret" is a certainty. This archangel was the representative on earth of the hidden Jewish God Michael in short.[16]

Clearly, Osiris was but another name for that person known in the Americas as Quetzalcoatl, Kukulcan, and Votan who, together with his six companions, appears to have been commemorated at the Temple of the Seven Dolls at Dzibilchaltun, in the Yucatan, which is named after seven figurines found deposited there.

On the 19 January 1981, while visiting Gerry's family, I had the uncomfortable feeling that someone was watching me from the far side of the room. The same had apparently occurred to Gerry, for I saw that we were both staring in the same direction.

"We have a visitor," said Gerry. "It is the white-robed spirit-guide, and he is indicating that he wishes to tell us something. Yes," continued Gerry, "he is asking me to say that when the craft of the Travelers was approaching earth, it resembled a huge comet with its tail stretched across the sky."

"That makes sense," I replied, "for in some parts of the ancient world, early people built disc-shaped enclosures attached to serpentine avenues; and what is more, I recently read that when the Aztecs saw a comet, they thought it was the return of a certain 'star serpent' that was involved in earth's earlier history."

Over the following months, I found that the Japanese Ainu worship a serpent that once descended from the heavens. The Druids revered the serpent and its egg. The serpent they believed formed itself into a ball that was hurled into the air. In Ohio, in the United States, stretched over a quarter of a mile, appears the largest serpent mound in the world, with coils extended in seven curves. Protruding from its mouth is a large oval object thought to represent an egg.

So far, we have considered the seven-stemmed Jewish candlestick (the menorah), seven-headed serpents, and groups of seven serpents, all of which clearly symbolize the same objects. The sacred tree is another like symbol, the Asian Shamanistic version of which is seven-branched and represents the seven levels of heaven. In the British Museum there is an early Middle Eastern drawing showing two human figures with arms outstretched toward such a tree, presumably in adoration.

In a legend from Nias, Oceania, it is said that long, long ago a limbless, headless object appeared. From this descended a tree from which came a party of gods.

While excavating a tomb in Monte Alban, Mexico, in 1931, Alfonso Laso discovered an incised jaguar bone that portrayed the birth from a tree of Quetzalcoatl. The Kayans of Borneo, who also revere seven deities, add that their ancestors issued forth from a tree that came to rest on earth after descending from the heavens. Irish legend and Sanskrit lore tell of seven holy trees. In A.D. 1132, monks who practiced the occult arts, built, near the banks of the River Skell in England, the Benedictine Fountains Abbey in whose foundations they planted seven yew trees. Several hundred years later, there stood in a north London road a circle of seven huge elm trees. This road is now known as Seven Sisters Road. Across the seas in Mexico, Chichen Itza was formerly known as "Uucil-abnal" (seven bushes). The oak tree was revered by the Aryans who regarded it as their chief god. Can it be coincidence there are at least six places called "Siebeneichs" (seven oaks) in Germany, and a Sevenoaks in Kent, England?

On 12 December 1979, after Quatal told of his visit to one of the seven stars, I asked Gerry if he had been aware of anything while in trance. He told me he had found himself in an Indian village in which there were several discs, each standing on three legs.

"That is interesting," I said, "for the three-legged emblem and pottery appeared in many parts of the ancient world."

Three years later, I found another bookshop specializing in the occult. Knowing this would be of interest to Gerry, I mentioned it to him and we arranged to visit it together.

Gerry spoke to the owner, while I glanced through the books. The first book I looked at contained a chapter concerning spiritual ascent, including the Buddhist belief in seven heavens. As the remainder of the book was of no interest, I replaced it on the shelf and, in so doing, noticed a book by Elizabeth Van Buren, entitled *Lord of the Flame*. I opened it at random and was fascinated to read that a picture had been discovered of seven three-limbed discs and an eighth winged disc.[17]

It was a cold winter's evening, and I was sitting in my study reading about the ancient city of Babylon when it suddenly occured to me that this city was reputed to have been built on seven hills. "Interesting," I thought, "for the same is said of Jerusalem, Rome and Istanbul."

Not long after, the Book of Revelation, chapter 17, verse 3 confirmed another piece of my puzzle was falling into place: "So he carried me away in the spirit into the wilderness: and I saw a woman sit upon a scarlet coloured beast, full of names of blasphemy, having seven heads."

L. Farra. Photo by Stephen Farra.

"The seven heads are seven mountains," explained my source. On reading this passage, it occurred to me that it resembled parts of the Gospel of the Essenes and the following text from *The Book of Enoch:* "And beyond that abyss I saw a place which had no firmament of the heaven above, and no firmly rounded earth beneath it; there was no water upon it, and no birds, but it was a waste and horrible place. I saw there seven stars like burning mountains."[18]

I noted that in similar writings to the Book of Revelation, the Gospel of the Essenes tells of a woman clothed with the sun, bearing a crown of seven stars on her head. Clearly, the "seven heads" were "seven mountains" (known as seven stars). So far as the "beast" is concerned, Rev. 17:11 explains, "he is the eighth."

In an ancient Sumerian legend, the hero, Lugbanda, on one occasion crosses seven mountains, and in another tale he is involved in an adventure with seven heroes.

The Israelites acknowledged a sacred mountain called Zion. Although the origin of this name is unknown, it is interesting to note that it similar to the Hebrew word *zayin*, which means seven.

The Incas had a holy hill that they called Tampu-Tocco. From this, they claimed, came Manco Ccapac, the first Incan ruler, who had seven brothers and sisters.

In Asia, there are legends of a seven-tiered mountain called Meru. The ancient Persians taught that this was the home of seven gods, and the Hindus say that on it are the seven celestial Rishis from whom they claim descent.

In a tale told in the Altaic region of Asia, Meru is claimed to have been a "golden mountain" that once descended to earth carrying the creator.

Chapter Four

In the Koran, the Moslem holy book, there appears a version of the legend of the seven sleepers. This tells of seven men who, for more than 300 years, lay in a deep sleep in a cave, at the entrance of which slept their dog. On reading this myth and others in *The Horse in Myth and Magic*, it occurred to me while that, as already appears, the "seven stars" are symbolized as mountains, how better than to describe their interiors as caves, and how more appropriate for people living long before the space age to tell of seven men enduring a prolonged period of sleep in a cave.

The Mexican Zoques Indians say that the great god Condoy once came to earth and, after emerging from a cave in a high mountain, stayed and taught them civilization. When it was time for him to go, Condoy returned to his mountain and entered the cave. The door of the cave then closed, and the god departed on a civilizing mission to other parts of the world. Although the mystical seven does not appear in this legend, it does in many relevant others.

The Ashantis, in Ghana, believe that the first seven men emerged from holes in the ground accompanied by some females, a leopard, and a dog. For the purposes of our story, the females and leopard can be disregarded. The dog, however, will be returning in due course.

In ancient Babylon, there were legends of "seven genii" who lived in holes in the ground. In Mithraism, it was claimed that Mithra owned a cave with seven doors and seven altars; and in Zoroastrianism, Zoroaster was said to have lived for seventy-seven years, seven of which were spent in a cave.

When the Travelers arrived on earth, Quatal stated that they were dressed in close-fitting, gold-colored garments and carried staffs. When they emerged from their craft, their bodies radiated heat, and when some of the Indians went too close, their skin was affected.

In Teutonic mythology, Mimer's seven sons dressed in wondrous clothes, and fell asleep in a fabulous room. On a wall in this room hung seven swords that only the seven sons could use. Those who went too near to the sleepers found that their limbs had withered.

The seven sleepers of Epheaus were seven Christians sentenced to death, but they had cunningly managed to escape and hide in a cave for 360 years. In an eighth-century legend, seven men dressed as Romans fell asleep in a cave in West Germany. A man who discovered them there tried to remove one of their garments and, while doing so found, to his horror, that his arm had withered.

In *The Horse in Myth and Magic*, M. Oldfield Howey relates a legend that claims that the Earl of Mullaghmast lies in a deep slumber in a cave with his soldiers and their horses.[19] Every seven years, the Earl and his horse are said to awaken and travel around Currough of Kildare.

Celtic mythology says that Finn, one of seven men who was renowned for his fair hair, was taught science and how to use a magical spear by an elderly sage. One night a beautiful woman named Saba appeared to him. Finn fell in love with her and they married and departed for seven days. Unfortunately for poor Finn, his wife deserted him, and he spent seven years looking for her. Later, Finn and his six companions fell into a deep sleep in a "magical cave." With these seven Celtic sleepers was Finn's dog.

When Layard, the renowned archaeologist, was excavating at Babylon in the Nineteenth century, he reported that it was not unusual for travelers in the Middle East to have Arabs point out local caves in which the seven sleepers endured their many years of sleep.

Long ago, says a North American Zuni Indian myth, the Zuni were visited by the god Paiyatuma and a party of seven white-robed corn maidens who were carrying magical staffs. After a while the villagers were enchanted to hear music coming from a cave in Thunder Mountain and sent messengers to investigate. Inside the cave, the messengers were amazed to discover Paiyatuma with a second group of seven maidens who were also carrying magical staffs. This second group of maidens are said to have resembled the first, just as the "House of Seven Stars" resembles its reflection in the waters below. Paiyatuma then played his flute, a drum sounded, and a thunderous noise ensued, whereupon the whole cave vibrated and flames, which were issuing from it, emitted a white mist. It was then that the seven maidens entered their bower, removed their white robes, laid down their staffs, and departed.

We have seen that these various legends associate seven men and, as we have seen in the last example, seven females with a cave. Since, however, several sources make reference to seven mountains, it should come as no surprise to find that others tell of seven caves.

Near Alexandria, in Egypt, at the time of the Ptolomies, a huge burial enclosure was hewn out of the rocks. This took the form of a wide central passage surrounded by seven huge chambers.

Buddhists tell of a cave with seven rooms; while according to the Maya, Toltecs, and North American Hopi Indians, their ancestors came forth from seven caves. Similarly, the Aztecs claimed that their people were part of seven migrations from seven caves on a journey that commenced in "Atzlan."

Earlier in the book we noted that the Torajas of Indonesia tell of the sudden appearance of seven mysterious objects. They also say that, after these arrived, a ladder extended from one of them and it was possible to climb it and speak to God.

Tibetan sources refer to the arrival of seven heavenly thrones and of seven kings who descended to earth on a ladder. Most of the world's religions acknowledged seven worlds, heavens, or spheres, each of which was ruled by one of a group of seven divinities.

The ancient Persians taught that god sat on a throne in the highest of these and that man was only allowed on earth, which was the lowest. The Hindus also believe that earth is the lowest of the seven worlds, which coincides with the Buddhist belief in a physical plane surmounted by six spiritual levels. The seven levels of heaven are also acknowledged by Siberian peoples, some of whom claim that the lowest level is inhabited by certain beings who once came down to visit earth.

The African Dogon use various face masks in their rituals, and one of these symbolizes the seven worlds. The African Bambara believe that life spans seven ages, and these they associate with the seven skies.

In the apocryphal work *The Ascension of Isaiah*, Isaiah is taken to the seven heavens, where he sees Enoch. Enoch, as we have noted, is claimed to have risen above the earth in the company of seven white men. He is also said to have seen seven groups of angels led by the seven archangels.

Moses, we are told, beheld the seven heavens after ascending Mount Sinai to meet the Lord. In the Jewish festival of Pentecost, it was customary to bake loaves of bread in the form of seven rings. These symbolized the "seven spheres" sent down by the Lord when he gave the law to Israel.

The Koran says that the seven heavens are solid and that Mohammed was taken to them by an angel. Similarly, Christianity claims that it was to these seven heavenly halls that St. Paul was escorted by an angel. In the seven heavens were the lesser angels and the seven archangels, the greatest of whom was Michael, the emisary of the Lord.

In *Myths of the Americas*, Brinton, quoting Torquemada, says that traditionally, the seven caves of the Central American Indians were ruled by the seven creator gods who were associated with the pyramid of Chohula.[20] This pyramid was dedicated to Quetzalcoatl/Votan[21], who led seven families and was "Son of the Lord of the Seven Caves."[22]

The Olmecs of Central America claimed to have been of the seven peoples who originally populated the earth and who emerged from seven caves.[23] Similarly, the Brahmins of India, who claim to be descended from the seven celestial Rishis from the sevenfold Mount Meru, are divided into seven groups.

Chapter Five

It was a hot day in August 1981, and I was standing on the top of the massive Pyramid of the Sun, admiring the breathtaking view of the remains of the city of Teotihuacan some thirty miles from Mexico City. It had certainly been a most exhilarating morning. At 9:00 A.M., our party had left the hotel in Mexico City to join the waiting coach outside, which, to my astonishment, was decorated on either side with a painting of a huge serpent.

Our first important stop that morning was at the Shrine of the Lady of Guadeloupe, which is the holiest place in Catholic Mexico. Outside the cathedral, we had seen the pilgrimage of men and women arriving on their knees; some of these people, we were told, had traveled great distances in this uncomfortable manner.

After leaving the cathedral, we enjoyed the beautiful views of Mexican countryside, with its occasional glimpses of luxury contrasted with extreme poverty. At last, we arrived at Teotihuacan, where, together with our guide, we visited the Temple of Quetzalcoatl, around whose various levels the bodies of serpents presented themselves, while, on the upward slope, a series of serpent heads grimaced at the parties of tourists.

Leaving the Temple of Quetzalcoatl, we climbed aboard the coach and, after a short journey, arrived at a long, broad avenue lined on either side with numerous small temples and dominated by the colossal pyramids of the sun and moon. With some effort, I climbed the narrow steps of the former, and there I stood enjoying the wonderful view from the top, wondering just what sort of ceremonies had taken place here in the distant past.

While looking through my binoculars at what had once been one of the largest cities in Central America, I recalled that when astro-archaeologist Gerald Hawkins had tested Teotihuacan for astronomical alignment, he discovered that its main westerly pointing road was aligned to the Pleiades, the main road to the north, to the brightest star of Ursa Major and the eastern alignment to Sirius (one of the seven stars of Canis Major).[24] It also came to mind that the people of the Teotihuacan had constructed, beneath their city, "seven caves" in the form of seven-headed serpents of India, Cambodia, and Sri Lanka. This city, I pondered, was aligned to various stars, all of which are connected with the number seven and, what is more, the seven caves were of significance to its people. Having descended to earth from the heavens, what could be more appropriate to symbolize the seven craft with than groups of seven stars.

On my return to England, I discovered that the constellations of Ursa Major, Ursa Minor, the Pleiades, Orion, and the seven planets feature prominently in numerous ancient religions.

Blavatsky clearly understood that there was a special reason for this but was unaware of a deeper meaning when she wrote:

The now universal error of attributing to the ancients knowledge of only seven planets, simply because they mentioned no others, is based on the same general ignorance of their occult doctrines. The question is not whether they were, or were not, aware of the existence of the later discovered planets, but whether the reverence paid to them, to the four esoteric and three secret, great gods—the star angels—had not some special reason.[25]

The writer ventures to say that there was such a reason, and it was this:

Had they known as many planets as we do now (and this question can hardly be decided at present, either way), they would still have connected only the seven with their religious worship, because these seven are directly and specially connected with our earth or using esoteric phraseology with our "septenary ring of spheres."[25]

Just as each of the seven stars of the Travelers appears to have had its own leader so, according to the Greeks, Romans, Indians, and Sabeans, each of the seven planets had its own god. Similar beliefs persisted well into the Christian era, for as late as the sixteenth century, Pius V issued a papal bull allowing the Spanish to worship the "Seven Spirits of God," adding that "One could never exalt too much these seven rectors of the world, figured by seven planets."

Some four hundred light-years from earth are the estimated two hundred and fifty stars of the Pleiades, seven of which have received a prominent place in religion and mythology in every part of the world. The Pleiades, the legends explain, were associated with massive upheavals and floods that once took place on this planet and were the home of certain gods who once visited earth.

While I was visiting Merida, in the Yucatan in Mexico, I was most fortunate in being able to acquire two books written by Jose Diaz-Bolio (*Instructive Guide to the Ruins of Chichen Itza* and *Ruins of Uxmal*), who has spent twenty-seven years researching the religion of the Maya. From his study of their art and buildings, this learned gentleman concludes that the rattlesnake and its "rattle" were the most important of Mayan symbols and that the serpent is closely linked with the creator. What he does not mention, however, is that to the Maya, the rattler's rattle symbolized the Pleiades—a constellation that they believed was once involved with a catastrophic earth upheaval.

The Maya, however, were not the only Central American people to attach such importance to the seven sisters. The Aztec calendar was based on a fifty-two–year cycle and, when this was drawing to an end, the people trembled in fear, anticipating that the earth was about to be destroyed by catastrophic earthquakes. On the last day of the cycle, Aztec priests climbed to the top of the special mountain and there, at night, they waited for the Pleiades to reach their zenith. When this occurred, a prisoner was sacrificed, and the people rejoiced that life would continue for at least another fifty-two years.

Groups of seven stars featured prominantly on Babylonian monuments and seals and, according to Layard, the walls of the southwest palace of Nimroud were ornamented with "seven discs," suggested by him to represent either the Pleiades or Ursa Major.[26]

At Nasca, in Peru, spread over a wide area in the desert, are mysterious drawings and lines that Maria Reiche has studied for much of her life.

"Using a star-chart given to her by Paul Kosok," says Tony Morrison, "she has spent years calculating all the rising and setting points of stars in relation to the direction of lines—or the edges of large cleared features. Her conclusion was that a great number of lines and triangles coincided with the rising and setting points of the group of stars known as the Pleiades or Seven Sisters."[27]

On being questioned on the significance of the Nascan

lines, the local Indians explained that they were "Pathways to the Gods," this being in line with a pre-Inca legend that says that gods from the Pleiades once visited earth.

In *Atlantis and the Seven Stars*, J. Countryman says that the Pleiades may well have been connected with the origin of Atlantis and that earth might have been visited by beings from that constellation.[28]

Earlier this century, American psychic Edgar Cayce forecasted that part of the remains of Atlantis would be discovered at Bimini in the Bahamas.[29] In 1968, what appeared to be huge stone walls were found beneath the sea at Bimini, and six years later, Professor David Zink, assisted by American psychic Carol Huffstickler, commenced a series of investigations into the site. In *The Stones of Atlantis*, Professor Zink not only relates the results of his fascinating study, but also reports the incredible claim by Miss Huffstickler that earth was seeded by a cosmic race from the Pleiades.[30] This provides an interesting backing to a claim made by first century B.C. writer Diodorus Siculas, that the Pleiades lay with the heroes and gods and became the ancestors of mankind.

The Book of Zechariah in the Bible describes the seven candlesticks as the seven eyes of the Lord. In Polynesia, the Pleiades are known as "the seven eyes of heaven." The Maoris call them the left eyes of seven great leaders, and the Hawaiians refer to them as Makalii, after a god who came to earth from that constellation.

Two *i*'s commonly end Polynesian words and, if removed, in this case present us with the name Makal. Makalii was also known to the Hawaiians as Koko. On Easter Island, Ku-ku-u is stated to have been one of the seven initiates who first discovered the island, and Kukulcan, to the Maya, was the white-bearded god otherwise known as Quetzalcoatl. The word "can" attached to the

Huge "winged, bearded-man bull" from the gateway of King Assurnasirpal's palace at Nimrud. Photograph by L. Farra. Courtesy of the British Museum.

end of this name means serpent. Incidentally, to the Celts, Cu Chulain was a fair-skinned man who had seven pupils in each eye and traveled around the world with a huge fiery wheel.

Bear cults are found among the Japanese Ainu and peoples of northern Asia and northern America. Although the Ainu regard the bear as their chief god, some explain him as not being god himself but his messenger, who once came down to earth in human form. The deeper significance behind this belief becomes clear when we find that to the peoples of the Northern Hemisphere, the bear represents the seven stars of Ursa Major.

In India, some claim that the seven Rishas live on the sevenfold Mount Meru, but others suggest that they are to be found in the constellation of the Great Bear. Both of these places, however, clearly symbolize the same group of objects—the seven stars of the Travelers.

In India, Ursa Major was sometimes called "the seven bulls" and in ancient Egypt "the thigh" or "thigh of the bull." Special tombs were built for bulls in Egypt and, in the Egyptian burial service, the thigh of the bull was offered to Osiris, who was linked with these seven stars. The Sumerians revered the heavenly bull, and Assyrians depicted bulls with wings and beards. The ancient Egyptians, we recall, venerated the heavenly herd, consisting of a bull and seven cows. Another apparent version of this appears on a seventh-century jug in the Cyprus Museum, on which there is painted the rump of a bull decorated with seven concentric circles.

"It is of special interest to find," says Donald A. Mackenzie, "that the stars were grouped by the Babylonians at the earliest period in companies of seven. The importance of this magical number is emphasized by the group of seven demons which rose from the deep to range over the land. Perhaps the sanctity of the seven was suggested by Orion, the Bears, and the Pleiad, one of which constellations may have been the 'sevenfold' deity addressed as 'one.'

"At any rate," he continues, " arbitrary groupings of the stars into companies of seven took place for references are made to the Tikishi, the seven Lamashi and the seven Mashi, which are older than the signs of the zodiac; so far as can be ascertained these groups were selected from various constellations. When five planets were identified, they were associated with the sun and moon and connected with the chief god Hammurabi Pantheon. A bilingual list in the British Museum arranges the sevenfold planetary group in the following order:

"The Moon	—	Sin
The Sun	—	Shamash
Jupiter	—	Merodach
Venus	—	Ishtar
Saturn	—	Ninip (Nirig)
Mercury	—	Nebo
Mars	—	Nergal"[31]

Hammurabi's seven gods, it can now be noted, were said to have caused the flood, and one of them, Ninip, the messenger of the gods, was depicted as a bull.

We have seen that the peoples of the cold lands to the north adopted the bear and those of the Old World the bull to symbolize Ursa Major. In Central America, the Maya associated the number seven with the jaguar, and the Quiche-Maya gave the title "Balam" (jaguar) to three of their seven ancestors. The jaguar, like the snake, played an important part in the Mayan religion, and these fleet felines were often worshiped at shrines in darkened caves.

At the top of a winding stairway within the Pyramid

of Kukulcan in Chichen Itza in the Yucatan is a small room. In this room is the famous "red jaguar" statue whose back is adorned with a solar symbol. The Lencas of Central America tell of a flying jaguar. Legends in Peru tell of a jaguar that flashed through the heavens in the form of a star, and the Zapotacs say that their ancestors were born from a jaguar or bird that once descended from the heavens on the back of a "groups of stars."

When visiting Teotihuacan, near Mexico City, I noticed on the wall of one of the temples along the main avenue, the faded picture of what appeared to be a jaguar above seven circles. It seems likely that my understanding of this picture is correct, for, at Teotihuacan, there is a fresco depicting a jaguar/knight carrying a shield decorated with seven dots and an Aztec wood-carving portrays a jaguar, an eagle, and the six dots surrounding a seventh pattern that, to the Maya, symbolizes "god-seven."

When archaeologists were excavating the Olmec center at La Venta, in Mexico, they discovered a stela showing seven figures. The obvious leader of these is a bearded man carrying a staff or mace, and his six companions are jaguar/men. When Marion P. Hatch checked La Venta for astronomical alignment, he found that it was aligned to Ursa Major, whose outline is suggested to be reflected in the mouths of Olmec jaguar statues. Karl W. Luckert says that, "the Nuhua people (who include the Aztecs) called the jaguar 'Oceloth' and also used this name for Ursa Major."[32]

At Tiahuanco, near Lake Titicaca in Bolivia, is a ten-foot high gateway dominated by a central figure suggested to be Viracocha. The headdress of this person is decorated with the heads of six jaguars, and it brings to mind legends in Central America that tell how earth was once visited by jaguar/men from the stars.

Ivar Lissner says that the seven stars of Ursa Major have long fascinated the peoples of the Northern Hemisphere, who gave significance to the fact that they, together with various other stars, circle the polestar.[33] The Babylonians identified the polestar with the god Anu. Anu, to the ancient Egyptians, was the place where the gods dwelt, dressed in white robes and white sandals.

"One of the key patterns to be noticed in the pyramids," says Wm. R. Fix, "is that the main passage in almost all of them points toward the circumpolar stars around the celestial North Pole. From these facts," he adds, "it becomes clear that the ancient Egyptians were fascinated, one might say hypnotized, by the stars and by the circumpolar stars in particular. Whatever took place inside the pyramids had something to do with the circumpolar stars."[34]

The seven bright stars of Orion are made up of the three stars of the belt, plus four surrounding stars. The ancient Egyptians aligned one of the shafts of the Great Pyramid to Orion, and it is referred to in their pyramid texts and in the Bible. Orion is also of symbolic importance to the North American Hopi Indians, who, when its seventh central star is seen through the openings in their ceremonial kiva, sing seven songs.

At various times in earth's history, far-sighted people have tried unsuccessfully to persuade their fellow men to live in peace with one another. One such person was the deeply spiritual and remarkable Egyptian ruler Akhnaton, who, when he came to power, discouraged the worship of gods other than the Aton or Aten (the Lord). For this god, Akhnaton built a seven-roomed temple, and there he installed the god's symbol—a huge red disc. (Authorities have queried Akhnaton's reputedly having fathered "seven daughters." Possibly, this was an allegorical statement and had the same bearing as the "seven children" said to have been fathered by various biblical characters.)

The West African Dogon call the eighth and seven younger ancestors "Nommos." These ancestors are represented in the form of eight pillars extended in serpentine form around the symbols of the seventh. The eighth ancestor is distinguished from his seven companions by being the eldest. The seventh ancestor also has special significance, for it was "he" who helped civilize mankind. The arrival on earth of the first teacher or teachers would appear to be referred to in a Dogon tradition, which tells how Amma, the creator, sent a Nommo (the Instructors) to visit earth. According to the Dogon, while this Nommo was descending, its color was red, and it made a noise like thunder. When it reached the surface, it caused a great cloud or dust to rise, and its color was seen to change from red to white.

The Mayas of Central America worshiped red and white jaguars and claimed that when the seven Aphu arrived on earth, they took the form of men. Similarly, we have seen that the Dogon tell of red and white Nommos, describe certain Nommos as beings, and furthermore depict the heads of seven of them on one of their alter tabloids.

It seems, not without reason, that Jewish Cabalists tell of the seven heavens and seven kings in Edom, especially when we find that in Hebrew, *edom* means red. In addition, we should note that Seven Kumaras are said to have descended to earth in the Gobi Desert region within a "huge white star." The ancient Egyptians worshiped a bull called "Bukhe," which could change its color, and, the African pygmies say that god's messenger, Efe, arrived on earth, accompanied by a chameleon, which caused terrible storms. (The chameleon still causes fear among certain African peoples.) Red bulls were sacrificed in parts of the

Papyrus of Ankhef-N-Khons. Seven Egyptian gods in a boat.
Photograph by the author. Courtesy of the British Museum.

Old World, and Druids, dressed in long white robes, sacrificed white bulls, as did Romans and Egyptians. Sacred herds of white cattle were raised in England.

"On 6th April 1538," says Lewis Spence, "a certain Ellis Prince, incensed over idolatrous rituals in Wales, wrote the following letter to Thomas Cromwell, Secretary to Henry VIII:

There ys an Image of Darvellgarden within the said dioces, in who the people have so great confidence, hope and truste, that they cumme dayly a pillrammage unto hym, some with kyne, othir with oxen or horsis and the reste with money; in so much that there was fyve or syxe hundred the pilgrimes to a man's estimation, that offered to the said image the fifth daie of this present monethe of Aprill. The innocente people hath be sore aluryd and entised to worship the said image, in so much that there is a commyn sayinge as yet amongst them that who so ever will offer anie thinge to the said Image of Darvellgarden, he hath power to fetche hym or them that so offers oute of Hell when they be damned.[35]

"This idol," says Lewis Spence, "was conveyed to Smithfield and incontinently burned there, along with a friar or a priest who bore the same name as itself. The general circumstances surrounding the affair yield the impression that the idol was associated with a surviving cultus of the sacred red ox. Oxen were offered up to it and, as we shall see, the sacrifice of these animals was fairly common in Wales until a late date. An ancient British deity, known as 'Hue Gardarn,' was said to have drawn souls out of Annwn, or hell, and Darvellgarden had certainly some reputation in Wales as a saint. Darvell may perhaps be a corruption of *tarw*, the Welsh word for a bull."

The ancient Egyptians believed that on their journey into the afterlife, spirits addressed seven gods and passed

The Egyptian goddess Isis. Author's collection. Photo courtesy of Stephen Farra.

through seven gates into seven halls. At each gate, parts of a red bull, including "the thigh" (i.e., the symbol representing Ursa Major), had to be offered to the gods.

The Dogon say that the great teachers arrived on earth from the star-system Sirius. Sirius, the dog star, which was aligned to one of the main streets in Teotihuacan in Mexico, was also revered by the Egyptians, and it was later referred to in the Moslem holy book, the Koran, as were "the seven sleepers" and their dog.

Sirius, one of the seven stars of Canis Major, was claimed by the Egyptians to have had a ladder extending from it and to have been the home of certain deities. The Egyptians identified it with the goddess Isis, whom they often showed with wings and a disc. Isis, who was associated with the color red, was the seventh member of a group of gods to emerge from Anu. Since she was the wife of the great civilizing god Osiris, who himself was the seventh of a group of gods, it can now be seen that Isis the Egyptian mother goddess was the equivalent of the Dogon's seventh ancestor—the civilizer of mankind. Isis, it would thus seem, was a "flying red disc"—one of a group of seven.

A Chinese source says, "When the dark clouds covered the sky, everywhere at night a noise of thunder was heard in the north. This was what people call a descent of the celestial dog. It has the shape of a large moving star and produces a noise. When it descends and reaches the earth, it resembles a dog. Whatever it falls upon becomes a flaming fire. It looks like a fiery light, like flames, flaming up to heaven. . . . Thunder resounded in the northwest in a cloudless sky, and this was called a descent of the celestial dog. The celestial dogs live on top of a high mountain. Their color resembles that of a *wani-i* (crocodile dragon)."[36]

"In A.D. 637," writes W. Raymond Drake, "the Nihongi (book 2, page 168) reported:

A great star floated from the East to West and there was a noise like that of thunder. The people of that day said it was the sound of the falling star. Others said that it was earth thunder. Hereupon the Buddhist Priest, Bin, said: 'It is not the falling star but the Celestial Dog, the sound of whose barking is like thunder.'

"A week later there was an eclipse of the sun. The learned priest Bin was doubtless misled by *The Classics of Mountains and Seas*, a very ancient Chinese book, which said:

At the Heaven-Gate mountain there is a red dog called celestial dog. Its lustre flies through Heaven and as it floats along becomes a star of several tens of rods in length. It is swift as the wind. Its voice is like thunder and its radiance like lightning.

"This description," says W. Raymond Drake, "suggests a cigar-shaped spaceship. The celestial dog was Sirius, but this classical reference to a star which floated, elongated, glowing red, moved swiftly, sounded like thunder, and flashed radiation, parallels the great mother-ships seen high in our skies today."[37]

In Central America, dogs were associated with the "fire which descends from heaven," and Aztecs twinned Quetzalcoatl with such an animal. White dogs were sacred to the North American Iroquois Indians, who painted them with red dots, decorated them with feathers, and suspended them from trees in the belief that they would act as messengers to the great spirit.

An Aleut legend says that the Aleut came into being at the time when a certain being came to earth in the form of a dog. Another Aleut legend connects the origin of these people with "Makakh" (the mother dog) and an elderly man called "Iraghadakh." By removing the *kh*, that ends these names, and the first three letters of the latter, we discover Makakh and Ghada, which resembles Mikal and Goda.

The Dogon say that in addition to the Nommo that landed on earth, another, remaining in the sky above, had ten jetlike extensions from which came ten rays. Robert K. G. Temple suggests that this second "Nommo" was the parent craft of the one that landed.[38] I, in addition, believe that the latter was the eighth Nommo, otherwise known as the eighth ancestor.

In the Book of Revelation, in the New Testament, we read:

And there appeared another wonder in heaven; and behold a great red dragon, having seven heads and ten horns, and seven crowns upon his heads. And his tail drew the third part of the stars of heaven. (Revelation 12:3–4)

So far as the beast's ten horns are concerned, Revelation 17:13 says: "These have one mind, and shall give their power and strength unto the beast."

Other possible references to this "ten-horned" beast are found among the Hindus—who believe that Agni, the seven-armed god of fire, had ten mothers associated with ten fingers—and the African Bambara—whose traditions acknowledge the seven heavens and who use a face mask resembling an advanced flying craft with ten jets. The Israelites, incidentally, were instructed to blow the horn on the "tenth day of the seventh month," the sound of which is said to herald the return of the Messiah.

The red star Alderbaran was revered by certain ancient

people not only because of its color but because of its position between earth and the acknowledged seven stars of the Hyades that appear to surround it. In legend, Alderbaran was associated not only with the Hyades but also with the Pleiades. We have seen that when the Aztec's fifty-two–year cycle drew to a close, the people tensely awaited the arrival of the Pleiades, so that they could be assured life would continue for at least another cycle. Having sighted the Pleiades, the Aztecs began a twelve-day festival, at the end of which they scanned the skies in anticipation of the arrival of Alderbaran, whose appearance marked the time for offering human sacrifice. Although Alderbaran's significance to the Aztecs is not clear, it is of relevance that various ancient peoples associated it with the creator who once caused a devastating flood on earth.

Richard Hinckley Allen writes that the Hervey Islanders have a legend concerning Aumea (Alderbaran), the Pleiades, and Sirius, in which Aumea and Sirius are involved in a violent conflict on behalf of Tane.[39] Tane or Kane, the greatest of all Polynesian gods and ancestor of mankind, was a great white man who once came to earth and traveled around it carrying a long staff.

Chapter Six

Earlier in the book we saw that the spirit-guide Quatal told how the Travelers possessed multipurpose staffs that could heal the sick, make water flow from rocks, and cause other remarkable happenings. Replicas of these staffs have undoubtedly evolved through time into the magic wands of magicians, the sceptres of rulers, and the pastoral staffs of religious leaders.

More significantly, however, they are found in all parts of the world, linked with seven gods, such as the seven creator-gods in Central America and seven gods of happiness in Japan. They are also identifiable with the magical staffs or swords in the various versions of the Legend of the Seven Sleepers and with the staffs of the seven white-robed corn maidens in North American Zuni Indian myth. The African Ashanti say that when God was traveling around the earth, he was accompanied by an assistant who carried a magical staff and met seven men who had emerged from a hole. The Incas of Peru claimed that Manco Ccapac, their first ruler, came down from heaven in a golden wedge carrying a golden staff given to him by his father. A magical staff was also owned by the Celtic Manannan, who traveled on "three legs" in a craft that flashed through the skies over land and sea. Alchemist Basil Valentine referred, in his writings, to seven types of divining rods linked with the seven planets. The Catholic Church associates seven spirits with these seven heavenly bodies.

Thousands of years earlier, the Egyptian Papyrus Ani told of a crystal sceptre connected with "the thigh" (Ursa Major). Egyptian legend says that the Egyptian priests once owned a special staff that could levitate heavy objects, and just as models of tools have been discovered in some early burials, so small ivory sceptres were deposited by the Egyptians in the graves of the deceased for use in the afterlife.

"But lift thou up thy rod," said the Lord to Moses, "and stretch out thine hand over the sea, and divide it . . . And the children of Israel went into the midst of the sea upon the dry ground: and the waters were a wall unto them on their right hand and on their left." (Exodus 14:16,22).

A story similar to that of the Israelite exodus from Egypt appears in the Mexican *Annals of the Cakchiquels*, in which we are told how the seven tribes arrived at the seashore, hoping to see the land that they had been promised. With their staffs, the seven peoples then caused the waters to part, enabling them to cross over on the dry seabed. Likewise, in Celtic mythology, Thor received a magical staff from a giantess, and this he used when crossing a river. Once again, a legend from Africa tells how a Kaffir chief escaped the clutches of his enemies by parting the waters with his staff.

Exodus 17:6 explains that the wondrous staff given by the Lord to Moses could also be used for another important purpose: "Behold I will stand before thee there upon the rock in Horeb; and thou shalt smite the rock, and there shall come water out of it, that the people may drink."

In Peru, Viracocha, the staff-carrying creator-god, was reputed to have caused water to flow from the rocks; while in the Old World, the goddesses Rhea and Atlanta similarly struck rocks with their staffs in order to obtain water.

Manco Ccapac, the first Incan ruler, was stated to have placed his golden staff on the ground, whereupon it disappeared beneath the surface.

In Jewish legend, it is said that Moses' wondrous sapphire staff was first given by the Lord to Adam. Later, it passed through the hands of Jacob and Joseph until, eventually, it came into the possession of Jethro. Jethro then had a brilliant idea. He planted the staff in his garden and promised that whoever could pluck it from the ground could marry Ziporah, one of his seven daughters. When Moses saw Ziporah, he fell in love with her and, as he was able to remove the staff from the ground, he received her as his wife.

In a later Christian legend, Joseph of Aramathea is stated to have visited Glastonbury, in the west of England, with seven companions. There, he planted his staff, which took root. The Yoruba of West Africa add that god once sent to earth his son Oduduwa who had "seven sons." Oranyan, one of his sons who was associated with a snake, forced his staff into the ground, whereupon it turned into a pillar of stone.

It will be recalled that Quatal not only told of the amazing staff given to him by the Travelers but also referred to his gift of a special ring. Magical rings often associated with the mystical seven appear in legends and traditions. In Mithraism, for example, there were seven grades of initiate, the highest of whom was claimed to be god's representative on earth and whose symbols were a staff and a ring.

Quatal said that the staffs of the Travelers could be used for healing. The staff used as a symbol by the medical profession is derived from the one reputed to have been owned by Asclepius, the Greek god of medicine. Asclepius, a long-robed, bearded man who carried a staff encircled by a snake, was the son of the god Apollo who was linked with the number seven. Quatal also explained that the strange staff given to him by the Travelers could be used to contact them.

Vaughn M. Greene says that, according to Aztec legend, the gods on earth were able to communicate with those in the sky.[40] The Aztec-speaking Huichol Indians, who live in the mountainous region of southwest Mexico and who still retain their ancient traditions, use as one of their sacred symbols a staff called a "muwieri," which the Huichol ancestors are said to have used when they needed to contact the gods. Huichol shamans believe that the muwieri is still effective and use it in their rituals when they pray for rain.

The aboriginal Japanese Ainu use sacred staffs in their rituals relating to the bear. Sacred staffs feature prominantly in the religious lives of these people, who keep in their homes a special prayer staff called the "inau," which is believed to have the power to carry messages to god.

On 21 January 1981, while I was visiting Gerry and his family, we had a visit from the tall, white-haired, white-robed spirit guide mentioned earlier in the book. Until then, his background had been a mystery but, on this, his last visit, he informed Gerry that he had died in Egypt and that his remains had lain buried there for thousands of years. He then explained that, during his physical life, he had been a custodian and, although not elaborating on this, it seems likely that his duties were connected with the crystal staff that he carried, for he also said that one of the staffs of the Travelers had been left in Egypt, and there it was handed down from generation to generation. After some time its power waned and its use was forgotten.

Chapter Seven

A year before I met Gerry, a business associate who lived in Long Melford, in Suffolk, invited my wife Marianne and I to spend the weekend with his family. We arrived on the Friday evening after an uneventful journey and, having finished our meal, retired to the lounge where we sat discussing various matters of mutual interest until eventually the subject of ghosts arose.

Our host then said his house had been built on the site of a battle that occurred at the time of Cromwell, and a couple of weeks earlier his younger son claimed to have seen the upper part of the body of a cavalier walking past the open door of his bedroom.

For half an hour, the conversation continued on the subject of the afterlife, until our host asked whether either Marianne or I had ever used an Ouija board. I said that we had not but would be interested to see how it works.

Taking a sheet of white paper from his bureau, our host cut it into small pieces, and on these he wrote the letters of the alphabet and the numbers from one to ten. These were then laid in a circle around the table, and in the middle was set an upturned glass upon which we each placed one finger. At first nothing happened, but suddenly I sat up spellbound, for the glass began to move swiftly round the table. Then, it slowed down and began to spell out words.

"Read," it spelled out.

"Read what?" I asked.

"The Bible," came back the reply.

"What part of the Bible?" I queried.

"Genesis 6-2," wrote our unseen companion.

Taking a Bible from the bookcase, my friend opened it at the Book of Genesis, and, following instructions, read: "The Sons of God saw the daughters of men that they were fair; and they took them wives of all which they chose."

The meaning behind this statement remained a complete mystery, until the "Sherrick circle" meeting, in which Quatal told how some of the Travelers "had deposited their seed in the daughters of his tribe" so that great leaders would be born.

According to the Incas, giant men once descended to earth and mated with their women. In a legend of the African Ashanti, it is said that long, long ago god created seven men who descended to earth on a chain, fathered children with earth women, and then returned to the heavens. In a Chinese legend, it is said that a cowherd married one of seven fairies who, after giving birth, returned to heaven. The North American Blackfeet Indians tell of a man who fell in love with and took as his wife one of the seven sisters in the sky, while an Australian aboriginal tale relates how a man courted and married one of seven sisters, who later rose high into the heavens where they became the Pleiades. A South Seas tale tells how a man mated with a beautiful woman from the "seventh heaven" and the Quiche-Mayan Popul Vuh refers to a maiden who conceived after saliva from the seven Aphu fell on her. Equally fascinating is a reference on page 371 of the Hibbert lectures; "Seven Kings, bretheren, appeared and begat children 6000 in number were their peoples. The God Nergas (death) destroyed them."[41]

It was on 10 January 1980, that I was at a meeting of the "Sherrick circle." Gerry had been in trance and a series of trance communications had come through, but they were not directly connected with my research. However, just before Gerry came out of trance, he began to breathe heavily and seemed to be growing exceptionally tall. It was then that from his vocal chords came a deep gentle and sorrowful voice.

"We were the sons," it said. "We were left behind in the womb of the women. They called us giants. They said we were ugly. Oh! and how we cried for them who took our lives. And many many centuries after, did not another man cry: 'My God, for thou hast forsaken me.' "

Chapter Eight

While I was spending a social evening with Gerry in early 1980, he mentioned that he was aware of the presence in the room of T. C. Lethbridge, the late renowned archaeologist and psychic researcher. About an hour later, Gerry went into trance, his features and stature changed, and there before us sat a friendly, portly gentleman who introduced himself as Lethbridge. After complaining about Gerry's trousers, which were irritating his legs, our visitor told of his interest in dowsing, et cetera, and gave practical advice concerning this book.

Possibly two or three weeks later, while I was spending some time in the occult bookshop near my office, the name Lethbridge caught my eye, on a book called *A Step in the Dark*.[42] Taking it from the shelf and opening it at random, I found myself looking at a drawing of a giant hill figure discovered at Wandlebury in Cambridge, England. With astonishment, I saw that the ancient artist had drawn on the shoulder of this figure a huge serpent and a circle, enclosing six dots, surrounding a seventh. The pattern of six outer points set around emphasizing their center, which was briefly mentioned earlier, was of special importance in various parts of the ancient world. In Peru, houses were sometimes constructed in clusters of six, surrounding a central court and enclosed by an outer wall, and the Incan

Temple of the Sun, at Cuzco, is also said to have taken the form of six rooms set around a central courtway. The remains of a similarly planned temple has been discovered near Amman in Jordon. In ancient Israel, the city gates of Hazor and Geser were surrounded by six rooms, as was the gateway to the funerary temple of Knrepan in Egypt; and in the Book of Ezekiel in the Bible, Ezekiel is said to have visited a temple whose gateway was likewise constructed.

The North American Sioux Indians acknowledge the six cardinal points and the seventh central position. The same seven-point pattern is found in Aztec art and in the ceremonial kiva of the North American Hopi Indians, around whose circumference are six posts marking the cardinal points that surround a hole in the floor used for a special fire. (Also in the floor is another hole called a "sipapu," and this will be receiving our attention later.)

On the wall of the palace of Kapara, the Aramean ruler of Guzana-Tell Halef, archaeologists have discovered a relief in the form of a "winged disc" supporting several motifs, each bearing this same seven-point pattern. As we have seen, Donald A. Mackenzie, in discussing the Babylonian fascination with the number seven, mentions a sevenfold deity addressed as "One."[43] According to Professor Sayce, the name of this deity so frequently referred to in Babylonian records is god-seven.[44] This was also the name of the Central American Mayan Indian god who was symbolized by six points surrounding a seventh.

This unique Cretan Phaistos disc is covered on both sides with mysterious hieroglyphics that many have sought to interpret.[45] Professor Homet suggest that the disc may tell the story of the destruction of Atlantis. Although, to the sceptic, this theory may hold no water, it is interesting to note that one of the glyphs appears to be of a long-robed man, another of a staff encircled by a snake, and a third, repeated several times, is a disc enclosing six dots surrounding a seventh, which is suggested by some to represent the Pleiades.

The symbolic pattern of two interlaced triangles sometimes enclosing a central dot was used in various parts of the Old World and has also been discovered on the wall of a building in the Mayan complex in Uxmal, in the Yucatan, Mexico. Adopted by the Jewish people as their emblem, it has also come into Christian use. Thus, in such an exhibit, in the Benaki Museum, in Athens, Jesus occupies the seventh central position.

While visiting the earlier mentioned northeast London synagogue, I noticed that at the top of its flight of seven stairs leading to the ark hung a red lamp, close to which was suspended a huge fitment bearing seven circular lamps, six of which surrounded the larger seventh.

That this had special symbolic significance can be deduced from Rabbi Abbas, who is reported to have explained that "We are the six lights which shine from a seventh. Thou art the seventh light (the origin of us all), for assuredly, there is no stability in those six, save what they derive from the seventh."

"The six days of Creation," adds the Jewish Cabala, "revolve around the Sabbath. All nature circles around the seventh central position."[46]

When the Spanish first arrived in the Americas, greed had them chasing an elusive "golden man" who, unbeknown to them, had departed thousands of years before their arrival. Hearing of the fabulous "seven golden cities of Cibola," they set off in search of hoards of gold. Unfortunately, for them, all they found were the seven villages of the North American Zuni Indians constructed in a cluster of six surrounding the seventh, reflecting the Zuni's reverence of six lights surrounding the seventh.

Chapter Nine

On 10 February 1980, Gerry opened the front door of his home, to be confronted by the figure of a mustached man dressed in cowboy clothes and a large cowboytype hat. The unexpected "spirit-visitor" introduced himself as Colonel Fawcett and, without giving an explanation, showed him a map of Bolivia; then he vanished, but returned three days later, to tell Gerry to inform me that I should research Bolivia, where I would discover material for my book.

A few days later, while I was once again in a bookshop, I noticed a book titled *Exploration Fawcett* and, with Gerry's recent visitor in mind, decided to purchase it. The book told of Fawcett's explorations in South America and his belief in lost cities in its jungles. It also tells of an image about ten inches high, acquired by Sir H. Rider Haggard in Brazil, and then given to Fawcett. In order to discover its background, Fawcett took it to a psychometrist who gave him the following astounding reading:

I see a large irregular shaped continent stretching from the north coast of Africa to South America. Numerous mountains are spread over its surface and here and there a volcano looks as though it is about to erupt. The vegetation is prolific and of a tropical or subtropical nature.

On the African side of the continent, the population is sparse. The people are well formed but of varied nondescript class, very dark-complexioned though not negroid. Their most striking features are high cheekbones and eyes of piercing brilliance. I should say that their morals have much to be desired and their worship borders on demonology. I see villages and towns revealing signs of fairly advanced civilization and there are certain ornate buildings which I take to be temples.

I seem to be transported across the country to the western side. Here, the vegetation is dense, the flora gorgeous and the inhabitants far superior to the others. The country is hilly and elaborate temples are partly hewn from the faces of the cliffs, their projecting facades supported by beautifully carved columns. Processions of what look like priests pass in and out of these temples and a High Priest or leader is wearing a breastplate, similar to the one on the figure I am holding. Within the temples it is dark, but over the altars is the representation of a large eye. The priests are making invocations to this eye and the whole ritual seems to be of an occult nature coupled with a sacrificial system, though whether human or animal I cannot see.

Placed at various parts of the temple are a few effigies like the one in my hand—this one was evidently the portrait of a priest of high rank. I see the priest take it and hand it to another priest with instructions to retain it carefully and in due course deliver it to an appointed one who, in turn, must pass it on until at length it comes into possession of a reincarnation of the personage it portrays, when numerous forgotten things will, through its "influence" be elucidated.

The teeming population of the western cities seem to consist of three classes: the hierarchy and the ruling party under an hereditary monarch; a middle class; and the poor, or slaves. These people are absolute masters of the world and, by a great many of them, the black arts are practised to an alarming extent.

I hear a voice saying, "See the fate of the presumptuous." They count the Creator as under their influence and subject to their powers but the day of retribution has come. Wait and watch.

Then I see volcanoes in violent eruption, flaming lava pouring down their sides and the whole land shakes with a mighty rumbling sound. The sea rises as in a hurricane and a huge portion of land on both east and west disappears under the water, leaving the central part flooded but visible. The majority of the inhabitants are either drowned or destroyed by the earthquakes. The priest to whom the effigy was given rushes from the sinking city towards the hills where he places the sacred charge in hiding, then continues his flight eastwards.

Some of the people accustomed to the sea take to boats and sail away; others escape to the central mountains, where they are joined by refugees from the north and south. The voice says, "The judgment of Atlanta will be the fate of all who presume to deific power."[47]

On 23 May 1980, while I was visiting the Sherrick family, Gerry's eldest son, Shaun, asked whether it would be possible to obtain further evidence in support of the psychic material already received. Shortly after that, Gerry went into trance, and we found ourselves in the company of a wild man who swung his arms round and spoke in a gruff voice.

"Listen, listen well," he said, "because we will not repeat these words again. Because the medium has worked for us well, we will give you knowledge. Listen well, you who doubt. You who wish to know. I lived on the magic island. The magic island. The magic island you know as Ireland. Do you understand? You take away the word 'magic;' 'island' you understand? We were a wild people. We ate the flesh of other people. You understand? North, you understand? I speak in your tongue, my brother. [This remark was addressed to me.] North by northwest. North to where the ice and snow is. You understand? Down, down, to what you now call, how you say this word? Azores Islands. You understand? We stand and we see water come and we see a land sinking. North down, great lands sinking.

"We hear you say 'proof,' 'proof,'? We did not have proof. Only what we see with our own eyes. You understand? If you do not want to believe what comes from the mouth of the instrument, that is up to you. We saw a great land destroyed. The land was north, from the snow, down to the warm climate and where you now have your ocean, which you call the Atlantic Ocean. One land mass. You understand?"

"Did you know the name of that land?" I asked.

"We did not know what this land was called," he replied, "because we did not travel over to it. But, my brother, when I was a boy, from this land came flying birds that would come down and take my people, and we were afraid and these birds that came down made terrible sound and they came and dug up our earth and took our rocks away. I witnessed the destruction of this land."

I then asked whether he knew what had caused the destruction.

He replied, "All I know, my brother, is that there were great waves, much thunder and lightening. Much of my island was also submerged and many of my people perished. I believe I also perished but I cannot remember so clear. But a little while before the island went, great birds came down. So long ago! So long ago! But there was a story told of one man and his family who survived, but it was so long ago! So long ago!"

In August 1981, while visiting the temple of Akib-Dzib at Chichen Itza, in the Yucatan in Mexico, I recalled that James Churchward had, in his writings, referred to the ancient building in whose strange darkened chamber I was now standing.[48] The guide lifted his torch, illuminating the lintel on the inner door, explaining that it was covered with undeciphered Mayan writing. I recalled, however, that Churchward had claimed that these told of the destruction of Mu—the homeland to the west.

An hour before visiting the Akib-Dzib temple, I was

fortunate to meet Professor Gualberto Alonzo and briefly discuss with him his book *An Overview of the Mayan World*, which I happened to be reading at the time.[49] People who visit the Yucatan are often struck by the remarkable resemblance between the Maya and the Japanese. In his book, Professor Alonzo gives instances when people of the two races have discovered that they are able to converse with each other. Also, he told me that he had traced a now extinct people in India who appear to have been of the same race as the Maya and enthusiastically showed me an illustration of Babylonian pottery decorated with Mayan patterns.

The traditions of the Itza-Maya say that the Itza fled from their first homeland in the west, which was destroyed in a terrible flood, and that civilization was taught to them by a bearded god called Itzamna, who was associated with god-seven and various other deities.

Having a similar name to Itzamna is the staff-carrying god Izanagi, from whom Japanese emperors claim descent. Izanagi and his wife Izanami comprised the last of seven generations of gods and, as such, are identifiable with the Egyptian god Osiris and his wife Isis—the last of seven deities.

Various classical writers claimed that the gods became angry with the behavior of the Atlanteans, and therefore decided to destroy them. This is also suggested by Plato in his *Dialogues* in which he refers to terrible fire and destruction sent down from the heavens.

In the Quiche-Mayan Popul Vuh, it states that there was a time when men lived together in harmony and worshiped "Heart of Heaven" (god-seven). Due to the deterioration in man's behavior, however, Heart of Heaven caused a mighty flood on earth.

Various theories have been put forward to explain why

the pygmy peoples are found both in Africa and South America. Although academics tend to ignore traditions, the legends of the African pygmies may provide the answer to this puzzle. Long ago, say the pygmies, our ancestors lived in a large town, and all peoples were settled in one land and spoke one language. Then, God, a tall white-bearded man, sent to earth his son Efe, who was associated with a chameleon. There was terrible war on earth and in the heavens, followed by a devastating flood. This flood, it seems, was caused by God who, before leaving earth, struck it with a massive bolt of lightning.

Fawcett was convinced that there are lost cities in the jungles of South America, and many an explorer has reported seeing such remains.[50] In parts of North America, such as Death Valley, it is claimed that there are remains of cities that were subjected to such massive heat that they are barely recognizable. "There are a number of Indian legends" Hugh Cochrane explains,

> that tell of great shining cities of light that were located close to the Great Lakes. According to these stories, the inhabitants of these marvellous cities lived in great homes amid beautiful surroundings. It was from here that men were said to fly into the skies to meet the thunderbirds when they came down from the stars bringing ancient gods or great leaders. These legends also say that certain people were chosen from the tribes to accompany these space travelers back to the stars. Other stories tell of dark times on earth when the serpents returned to spread havoc over the land. It was during this time that the great cities were destroyed leaving nothing but ruin in their place.[51]

The Mayan Dresden Codex explains that the destruction of the world took place when a huge serpent appeared in the heavens and water poured from its mouth.

The Australian aboriginal Warrumga people claim that their ancestor was a huge serpent who, long ago, when there was much evil in the world, caused terrible destruction and killed many people. The Warrumunga drawings of this ancestor show it to resemble the huge serpent mound in Ohio, except that instead of an egg appearing between its gaping jaws there is a disclike object instead.

In caves at Prince Regent Valley, Fitzroy River, northwest Australia, you can see drawings of a "birdman" said to resemble those on Easter Island and to be connected with the rainbow serpent. In a nearby cave there again appears a drawing of a group of people being thrown backwards by a blast caused by an object descending from the sky. The sky is dominated by a huge serpent; below stands a bearded man with his staff pointing toward the upheaval.

Significantly, the ancient Egyptian Papyrus Ani told of a monstrous fire-breathing serpent named "Khali" that carried seven assistants on its back and attacked the enemies of the bearded, staff-carrying god Osiris.

In the *Book of Enoch*, Enoch's seven companions, presumably the seven archangels, were involved in putting an end to certain hostilities that were taking place on this planet:

And again I saw how they began to gore each other and to devour each other and the earth began to cry out loud.

And I raised mine eyes again to Heaven and I saw the vision, and behold there came forth from Heaven beings who were like white men; four went forth from that place and three with them. And those three that had come forth grasped me by the hand and took me up, away from the generations of the earth and raised me up to a lofty place and showed me a tower raised high above the earth, and all the hills were lower.

And one said unto me; "Remain here till thou seest everything that befalls those elephants, camels and asses and the stars and the oxen and all of them."

And I saw one of those four who had come forth first and he seized that first star which had fallen from heaven and bound it hand and foot and cast it into an abyss: now that abyss was narrow and deep, and horrible and dark. And one of them drew a sword and gave it to those elephants and camels and asses: and they began to smite each other and the whole earth quaked because of them. And as I was beholding in the vision, lo, one of the four who had come forth stoned (them) from Heaven.

Reports of similar events appear in the Book of Revelation, in the New Testament, and in the Gospel of the Essenes, except instead of white men stoning earth's wicked peoples, fiery destruction is sent down by seven angels causing earthquakes, floods, and the deaths of many men.

Most people know of the story of the biblical flood, but many are not aware that, according to Genesis 6:4; "There were giants in the earth in those days; and also after that, when the sons of God came in unto the daughters of men, and they bore children to them."

The "sons of God" taking wives from the daughters of men now needs no explanation, but what of these giants said to have lived at the time of the flood?

The ancient Anglo-Saxon epic of Beowulf tells how long ago the giants attacked the gods and were drowned on the instruction of the Lord in the boiling waters of a devasting flood.

In North America, the Montagnais Indians claim that God once lost his patience with the giants and, after advising a man to build a boat, destroyed them with a massive flood.

In Central America, the Cholula Indians say that there was once a land inhabited by giants that was destroyed by a flood. The same is found in China, where legends tell of a race of giant men who lived in a land of plenty that they lost through living wicked lives; and Aztec tradition tells how the jaguars destroyed an evil race of giants who lived in a past age.

The Greeks claimed that Typhon, one of the giants who made war on the gods, locked Zeus, the father of the gods, in a cave. Zeus was eventually released and a terrible struggle ensued, followed by a massive deluge. During these hostilities, his son Apollo fought with Python, Typhon's monstrous serpent son. So far as Apollo is concerned, let us note that his festivals were celebrated on the seventh day of the month, and that his other name "Ebdomais" (sevenfold), suggests that he was the Greek version of god-seven, especially when we recall that his son, Asclepius, the god of healing, was depicted as a long-robed bearded man who carried a staff.

Typhon or Set, as he was known to the ancient Egyptians, was said to have attacked and killed his brother Osiris. Osiris was later brought back to life, and his son Horus (often depicted as a hawk bearing a red disc) attacked and badly mutilated his wicked uncle Set.

In the Quiche-Mayan Popul Vuh, it says that "before the flood, there lived an advanced race of men who had a vast knowledge of the heavens."

According to the Jewish historian Josephus, Adam had a son named Seth, and he and his sons, who were good people, were very advanced in astronomy. After seven generations, however, they became evil and unjust toward their fellow men, and God, therefore, decided to destroy them with a flood. As Seth, Set, and Typhon appear to be one and the same, it is apparent that Set, the wicked brother of Osiris, was not a god but an advanced race of wicked men.

There was intense hatred toward Set in ancient Egypt and since he was claimed to be red-haired, as Donald A. Mackenzie explains, it was dangerous for children to be born with hair of that color:

Red-haired youngsters were disliked because the wicked god Set was red-haired and was likely to carry them away. Their mothers therefore had to exercise special care with them and there was a particular charm for their use. In Russia, red-haired people are believed to have more knowledge of magic than others and are disliked on that account.[52]

In Somerset, in England, red-haired people have long been associated with witchcraft, but in ancient Egypt feelings against them were so strong that they were likely to be burned and their ashes offered to Osiris.

When the Spanish arrived on Easter Island, they discovered among the islanders tall, white-skinned, red-haired men who artificially elongated their ears and who were said to be the descendents of the island's earlier race.

The Maoris say that their ancestors were in contact with an advanced race of red-haired people whose menfolk dressed in white robes. Presumably, there was some interbreeding with this people, for the Maoris, who are among the tallest people in the world, sometimes display the distinctive features of white skin and red hair.

The Hawaiians say that many, many years ago white men came to the islands, took wives from among the native women, and became leaders of their people. The descendants of these white men can still be found in the district of Ka'u on the main Hawaiian island. They are quite easy to recognize for they have light skin and red hair.

When the Spanish arrived in Peru, they discovered

among the Incan ruling class tall, red-haired white men who were referred to as the descendants of Viracocha.

The Incas also explained that when Viracocha destroyed an early evil race, he led some of the survivors to the area around Lake Titicaca. Near Lake Titicaca are the remains of the long-since deserted city of Tiahuanaco, built by a past race of master builders who are said, by the local Indians, to have been tall, red-haired white men who dressed in long white robes.

Brad Steiger writes,

Tiahuanaco, the "City of the Dead," flourished long before more intelligent members of the Incas decided to put one stone on top of another and fashion a crude hut. According to Incan legends, Tiahuanaco was built by a race of giants whose fatherland had been destroyed in a great deluge that lasted two months. These powerful survivors transported remnants of their culture to Tiahuanaco on the shore of Lake Titicaco, in Bolivia's high plateau. If Egypt was the principal colony of Atlantis in the Old World, then Tiahuanaco might well have been the sunken continent's attempt at rebirth in the New World. In his expedition of 1932, Wendell Bennet found evidence that the city is at least 5,000 years old.[53]

When the Spanish arrived in Peru, they discovered the remains of a highly advanced civilization that had long preceded the Incas and whose building techniques had clearly influenced the latter. Aqueducts stretched for distances of up to 150 miles; an advanced system of roads served the country, and thousands of feet up, in the Andes, at Tiahuanaco, were the remains of numerous pyramids and massive buildings, some of which had been constructed with the use of blocks of stone weighing as much as 200 tons. On the island of Coati, on Lake Titicaca, stood an important building resting on seven tiered terraces and at Tiahuanaco was the massive Gateway of the Sun, depicting forty-eight, winged, staff-carrying beings surrounding the staff-carrying figure thought to be Viracocha.

Thor Heyerdahl suggests that people from Peru fled to the Polynesian islands some fifteen hundred years ago. He also asserts that Easter Island was populated some fifteen to sixteen hundred years ago, the remains of which area he compares to those of Peru, particularly to the area around Tiahuanaco.[54] Says Constance Irwin:

Heyerdahl learned much more than that such a voyage was a physical possibility in ages past. He learned that on certain downwind Pacific Islands, old men still repeated ancient legends concerning the founder of their race, reputedly a bearded white chief-god named "Kon-Tiki."

Now, the name "Kon-Tiki" was an older form of a name already familiar to us in its Inca or Quecha version: Viracocha. In Peru, according to South American legend, the bearded white men who built the enormous stone edifices were, in time, attacked by a chief name Cari. Most of the white men were massacred, but Kon-Tiki/Viracocha and some of his friends escaped, fled to the coast, and presently disappeared westward over the sea. Thor Heyerdahl believes that Polynesian legends even yet extant are living proof that the bearded white men who fled Peru arrived safely in Polynesia. His theory is founded on evidence more substantial than legend, for here, on certain Pacific islands and atolls, where Kon-Tiki is still revered, are other appurtenances of his culture: pyramids, for example; also panpipes and helmets; and proof that irrigation, trepanning, and head deformation were practiced. Also, these same Pacific islanders knew that the earth was round.[55]

When the Europeans first discovered the Canary Islands, the population then consisted of a people of mixed race called the Guanches, some of whom were red-haired and white-skinned and over six feet tall. Physically, they are said to have resembled the last inhabitants of Tiahuanaco. On being questioned on their origins, the Guanches explained that their ancestors were the survivors of a catastrophic flood that destroyed their former homeland.

"Stones have been found in the Canary Islands," says Blavatsky, "bearing sculptured symbols similar to those found on the shore of Lake Superior. Berthollet was induced to postulate the unity of the early men of the Canary Islands and America. The Guanches of the Canary Islands were lineal descendents of the Atlanteans. This fact will account for the great stature evidenced by their old skeletons."[56]

The Zuni Indians in southwest North America often exhibit the features of white skin, blue eyes, and chestnut-colored hair. Zuni Indian legend says that "those above" repeatedly warned the Zuni about their bad behavior and eventually drowned many of them with a massive flood. When the deluge came, some of the Zuni fled to Thunder Mountain. (Thunder Mountain, we recall, was linked by the Zuni with seven white-robed corn maidens who carried magical staffs.) Harold T. Wilkins says that there have been many reported sightings of white Indians in the jungles of South America.[57] He also states that the Indians of Gran Chaco in Paraguay claim that their ancestors were visited by brilliant tall men who wore long white robes and came from the direction of Ecuador or eastern Peru.

Now, although Fawcett did not discover lost cities in the jungles of Brazil, what he did report was most relevant to our present subject. "There are white Indians in the Acre," this Frenchman told me. "My brother went up the Tahuamanu on a launch and was told that white Indians were near. He did not believe it and scoffed at the men who had told him but nevertheless went off in a canoe and found unmistakable signs of Indians. The next thing he knew he and his men were being attacked by big, well-built handsome savages, pure white, with red hair and blue eyes."[58]

"In India," says Donald A. Mackenzie, "there are legends of red-haired, red-bearded demon giants called 'Rakashasas.' Red-haired people," he adds, "are disliked in India as in ancient Egypt."[59]

Says Blavatsky,

The modern archaeologist though speculation ad infinitum upon the dolmens and their builders knows, in fact, nothing of them or their origins. Yet these weird and often colossal monuments of unhewn stones which consist generally of four or seven gigantic blocks placed together are strewn over Asia, Europe, America and Africa in groups or rows. They are found in the Mediterranean basin, in Denmark (among the local tumuli from twenty-seven to thirty-five feet in height), in Shetland and in Sweden where they are called ganggriften (or tombs with corridors); in Germany, where they are known as the giants' tombs (Hunengraben); in Spain and Africa; in Palestine and Algeria; in Sardinia, Malabar; and in India where they are called the tombs of the Dailyas (giants) and the Rakashasa, the demonmen of Lanka. That no giant skeletons have been hitherto found in the tombs is no reason to say that there never were remains of giants in them.[60]

The remains of huge men, some nearly eight feet tall, have been discovered in early British burials although not specifically in dolmens. It is interesting to note, however, that this form of burial has been discovered in Peru. Tiahuanaco's local museum is said to exhibit the skulls of huge men who lived in the area, and skeletons of very tall men have been discovered in rock tombs around Cuzco, the Incan capital. The remains of giant men have, in fact, been discovered in many parts of the ancient world, including Scotland, the home of some of Europe's tallest people, many of whom are red-haired.

In a bygone age, a race of master builders, using huge blocks of stone sometimese weighing in excess of 1,000 tons, carried out advanced building projects in the area of Ba'Albek in Lebanon. Although of unknown identity, legend says that the builders were of a race of giants who survived the flood.

Harold T. Wilkins says that according to ancient Babylonian records, astrology was taught to the Babylonian priests by giant men who survived the flood. These, he suggests were probably Atlanteans.[61]

Chapter Ten

"Something strange is happening," said Gerry. "I am getting the clear impression of a snake and of a huge man at least six feet tall. From the waist up he is bare and on his chest there is an breastplate fastened by a chain crossing over his shoulders. He is saying that his name is Ataman or Ozman and he is indicating that he wants to talk to you."

It was the evening of 24 April 1980, and I was visiting Gerry and his family. The evening had been pleasant and relaxing with a continuous flow of interesting conversation. Now, it seemed further information for my book would soon be forthcoming, for as I glanced at Gerry, I saw that he was going into trance.

"I am Atamon," boomed our visitor. "I am wise man. Nothing I don't know. I am priest of the temple of my gods. I have been asked by the guide White Cloud to come back in the body of the medium to speak to you.

"I lived in the great city of Atlanta. We grew prosperous. We learned many things. Your earth doctors and your earth scientists are but infants compared to the knowledge we possessed. You have on your earth psychic surgeons who perform operations without instruments and this we did on my plane when I was on earth.

"My people were good people but they were governed by ignorant and greedy people. And when the Travelers from the stars came to earth, they taught many things, but my people grew greedy for gain and, instead of producing a higher condition of living, they were more interested in filling their pockets and satisfying the desires of their physical bodies.

"When the Travelers left, they left with blessings, but they warned my people, 'Cease your wicked ways or we will destroy all that you possess.'

"Man from the star came. And he came to a good man. And he said to the good man, 'We will take you and your family away from the city, for we will destroy this city. But you will bring with you your family, and you will choose species of animals and creatures to bring out of the city.'

"So he came and he took the white-haired man and his family and the many animals and insects into the ship and they ascended into the heavens.

"And then there came great fires and waves so high. And I rushed to the temples of my gods and I prayed for them to take me with the star men. But the waters came. I drowned beneath the waves.

"Be warned. Be warned. This is coming to your earth. Great waves will cover your cities and your people will perish. But the star men will come once more and they will take with them men, and wives, animals. And once again it will be as it was in the beginning. When they return to the earth, the earth will be void, and the star men will make a new world.

"As it is written in your Bible, 'In the beginning,' so it will be once more 'in the beginning.' The Bible is not of the past but of the future. You do not read of the past, my friends, you read of the future. I have spoken. I shall not speak again."

Says Blavatsky,

Noah's Deluge is allegorical but it is not mythical, for the story is based on the same archaic traditions of men or rather of nations which were saved during the cataclysms, in canoes, arks and ships. No one would dare presume to say that the Chaldean Xisthrus, the Hindu Vaivasvata, the Chinese Peirun—the beloved of the gods, who rescued him from the flood in a canoe or the Swedish Belgamer for whom the gods did the same in the north, are all identical as a personage. But their legends have all sprung from the same catastrophe which involved the continent and the Island of Atlantis.[62]

In the Book of Genesis, in the Bible, it says that God looked down on earth and, seeing it corrupt, decided to destroy it with a massive flood. A wise and good white-haired man called Noah, however, was told by the Lord to build an ark in which he and his family would be safe. After his vessel was prepared, Noah set sail with the seven members of his family, seven pairs of every clean animal, and seven pairs of every species of bird. The ark rested on the seventh month, and after seven days a dove was sent out.

In 2 Peter 2:5, in the New Testament, it is said that God saved Noah, the eighth man. So far as the other seven are concerned, the Hindus claim that Manu, the first great teacher and mariner on the ark, was accompanied by the seven celestial Rishis, who were married to seven stars; while the Chaldeans believed that, at the time of the flood, Xisuthros was rescued and taken to the heavens together with the Seven Cabiri.

The ancient Egyptians claimed that when Osiris entered the ark, he took with him seven rays. In latter day Egypt, the ark of Osiris was symbolized by the seven stars of Ursa Major. Moving further forward in time, Musselmen also linked these stars with the flood era, for they called them the camel owned by Noah.

In the ancient Babylonian epic of Gilgamesh, Uta Napishtim, the mariner on the ark, tells his descendent Gilgamesh how the gods once decided to destroy the world with a terrible flood and how he was informed of their plan by the god Ea. Uta Napishtim explain that in order to survive the deluge he built an ark in the shape of a cube, with seven rooms in each of its seven levels. The terrible destruction continued for six days and ceased on the seventh, and the ark eventually landed on Mount Nisir, seven days after which Uta Napishtim sent out a dove to explore.

In a Mexican Indian deluge story, we are told that in the era of Coniztal (the white head), there was a terrible flood, and seven people took shelter in a cave. Likewise, a Toltec legend refers to seven men and their wives who took shelter in several caves.

In a Slavonian legend, we are told that everyone perished in the flood except an old man and his wife, who were advised to jump seven times on the rocks. Following this, the seven races were born, from whom the Lithuanians claim descent.

Again, a Peruvian legend explains that after the flood subsided, earth was re-peopled by seven Incas.

The ancient Egyptians claimed that when the sun god Ra decided to destroy mankind, he sent out Hathor in the form of an eye. This "eye" caused such terrible destruction that seven thousand jars were needed to collect the blood. This was then mixed with barley and emptied over the land, producing a terrible flood. (Stories in which waters turn to blood are not only found in the Bible but in many world deluge legends in South America. In the Amazon region, blood and water are associated with the Pleiades.) This however was no ordinary "eye," for another Egyptian legend says "that out of the pupil of the eye of Ra came seven wise men."

Hathor and Isis were obviously one and the same entity. Both were associated with Sirius; Isis was one of the group of seven deities, and Hathor was associated with the seven Hathors of the heavenly herd. Hathor and her priestesses owned seven jars, and replicas of these were kept at the Temple of the Sun near Babion in Egypt.

Seven jars are mentioned in the Book of Revelation in the New Testament, in which the seven angels empty their vials over the earth causing fiery destruction and the waters to turn to blood; while in a Chinese deluge legend, the empress Nu Kwa (not the similarity to the name Noah) fought the giants, who were responsible for the flood and presented offerings in seven vessels.

Tarot cards, used in fortune telling and believed to have been designed by initiates to preserve ancient knowledge, comprise four suites, one of which is staffs and another discs. One of the tarot cards depicts a large star and seven smaller stars, below which there is a female pouring water from a vase.

Polynesian tradition says the god Tangaro dwells in the "eighth heaven." Tangaro's sons are fair-haired, white men who once came to earth and helped civilize mankind and preached brotherly love. Tangaro had a wicked enemy on earth called Suqe and, although little is said of their conflict, the Polynesians believe that it was the former god who caused the flood.

The Cronica Mexicayotl tells of a rock in Quinhayan that had a cave in each of its seven sides. In Quinhayan, there were various species of wild animals and, from it, the Mexica emerged in pairs. This Mexican "Noah's ark" is called Chicomotoc (seven caves). The Quiche-Mayan Popul Vuh says that after the flood there was a period of torrential rain, fire, and darkness, during which panic-stricken people were prevented from entering certain caves due to the doors being closed. According to the Popul Vuh, this was the time people traveled to "seven caves."

Although the Itza Maya told of a lost homeland in the west, the Quiche and other Mayas believed that their ancestors came from the east, after a journey across the sea. Brinton, however, points out that, according to Mayan tradition, the Maya reached Central America in two streams—the main party from the east, led by the god Itzamna, and the one from the west, by Kukulcan, the Mayan version of Quetzacoatl.[63] Itzamna, it would seem, was either another name for Kukulcan, or else he was one of his "fellow gods."

The bearded god, Itzamna, and his fellow deities apparently used their special abilities to help the refugees reach the new homeland, for the Maya claimed that they were able to cross the dry seabed after the gods had parted the waters in twelve channels.

The African pygmies say that God (an elderly white man) once used a form of power to cause the waters to part.

In Aztec tradition, it is said that when the Aztecs departed from Atzlan, they arrived at the seven caves and rested. Some crossed the sea in boats, but for others a road was opened through the waters.

The Aztecs said that in the midst of the seas lived a giant earth monster on whose back "were created" and lived all the races of mankind. This evil beast became involved in a struggle with the god Tezcatlipoca, the god of destruction (known as Red Tezcatlipoca), who succeeded in defeating it after a violent conflict. Tezcatlipoca was said to have descended to earth in the form of a spider on a thread and was symbolized as the seven stars of Ursa Major.

Without doubt, Tezcatlipoca was another version of both the Mayan god-seven and the sevenfold Greek Apollo who also battled with those who sought to overthrow the gods.

The North American Apache Indians tell how they once lived in a great land, which was master of the world, but which was destroyed when the fire god sent down destruction. Many of the Apache were able to escape from the holocaust by fleeing through a tunnel built by star people.

In the Codex Vatanicus, we are told that, having destroyed an evil race of people, the god Tezcatlipoca, together with Quetzalcoatl, were helping to settle the survivors in a new homelands when they found their way blocked by an obstacle. Soon, however, they were able to proceed, for the gods constructed a subterranean tunnel.

Once again, traditions of the North American Hopi Indians say that after the gods destroyed the previous era, some of the Hopi were able to escape the carnage by traveling through hollow reeds.

The Quiche-Maya claimed that with them on an important journey was the "House of Stars," and the Aztecs told of being accompanied by the divine bird and its twice-seven companions. The Northwest American Athapascan Indians tell of a devasting flood when a thunderbird rescued their ancestors.

W. Raymond Drake says that, according to the Eskimos, their forefathers were transported by "great white birds" from lands devasted by flood, and they tell of beings with shining faces sent from the stars.[64]

The "Wild Irish Visitor" at the circle meeting said that, before the great land in the Atlantic sank beneath the waves, great birds came down. In *Prehistoric Germ Warfare*, Robin Collyins mentions an ancient Irish legend that tells of a time when huge birds sent down fiery destruction, and English tradition tells of the "Seven Whistlers," said to be seven birds associated with destruction.[65]

In a prophecy handed down from generation to generation by Yemenite Jews, it is said that one day huge birds would descend from the heavens and carry them to the Promised Land. In fact, several years ago, when many of them were flown to Israel, having never previously seen an aircraft, they thought that the ancient prophecy had come true. Incidentally, Yemenite Jews are said to physically resemble some North American Indians.

Although the origin of the aboriginal white Japanese Ainu is unknown, the Ainus claim that their ancestors arrived in the country after descending from the sky. Could it be that "seven stars," symbolized by the "bear," whom they worship, had some connection with this?

Some North American Indians say that long ago the great spirit sent to earth his messenger, Michabo (The Great White One). While he was here, there was much wickedness on earth that resulted in the "evil water spirits" being destroyed by a great flood. It is further said that, after this occurred, a huge thunderbird was sent ahead to search out new lands, and Michabo, who helped in their resettlement, became the ancestor of mankind.

Religious ritual songs and dances re-enacting the events surrounding the flood appear in widely dispersed cultures around the world. A song of the Lenni-Lenape Indians describes how long ago, when men were wicked and fought each other, a powerful snake, seeing their delinquent behavior, destroyed them with a flood, following which the "Great Hare" (Michabo) became the ancestor of mankind.

Taking part in a deluge ritual of the now-extinct North American Mandan Indians was a man whose body was painted white, and he was known as the "first man." When the first man entered the village, he told the Indians there had been a terrible flood and that he alone had survived in a boat. According to the Mandan, this first man was white, wore a long white robe, and carried a long pipe.

Chapter Eleven

The Holy One, blessed be his name, has successfully formed and destroyed sundry worlds before this one.
—Rabbi Abahu.[66]

The legend of the World Ages is found among American Indians, ancient Greeks, and many other cultures. This tells of a series of past epochs, each of which ended with massive earth upheavals, torrential rain, and floods. Although there is a variation in the number of eras, it is generally said that we are now in the fourth age.

American psychic Edgar Cayce told of three major upheavals in the history of Atlantis, the last of which left it submerged beneath the seas.

The Greeks taught that people of the first age lived lives of abundance, as did Adam and Eve in the Garden of Eden. The Hopi add that they were able to converse without speaking. The Hopi say that, after some time, the first peoples began to fight one another, and when God saw this he decided to destroy them. After terminating the age, God is said to have gathered the survivors together, and he led them beneath the earth's surface to take shelter with a subterranean people. When conditions were right, the refugees left their benefactors and made their way to the surface to establish the Second Age.

Both the Greeks and Quiche-Maya said that the people of this new age were physically weak, and the Hopi claim that they now began to use speech to communicate. In its earliest period, the second age is said to have been peaceful, but after some time, history repeated itself, and God terminated the age with a massive earth upheaval, causing a drastic change in climate.

The Hopi say that many people perished and that, once again, the survivors took shelter beneath the earth's surface.

When life returned to normal, the people went back to the world above and set about building the third age.

The North American Navaho Indians assert that it was in this new age that a great rattlesnake and seven other forms of snake appeared, and in Central America it was said that this was the time when the great white-bearded god came to earth and helped civilize its people.

All was not well, however, for, as the Hopi explain, people of this age built flying craft that they used to attack each other's cities. Clearly telling of the same events, the Quiche-Maya said that in the third age, Hunahpu, son of the seven Ahpu, visited earth and was involved in a violent struggle with the evil ones who were destroyed with an almighty flood.

The conflict between the gods and people of the third age is mentioned in the Quiche-Maya Popul Vuh and is re-enacted by the Central Amerrican Chorti Indians in a popular drama known as *The Dance of the Giants*. Taking part in this special play are actors representing a white giant, who is associated with the seven Ahpu, and a black giant (his opponent). Also, symbolically appearing are groups of seven stars and a sun king, whose cuffs bear "seven and ten" festoons, and whose golden hat terminates in ten points. At first, in this drama, the wicked black giant has things all his own way and boasts of having overcome "seven kings." Later, in the dramatic struggle between good and evil, the position is reversed, and the black giant suffers a resounding defeat.

In a Hopi Indian ritual called "Night of the Washing of the Hair," initiates gather in the darkened kiva, which is dimly lit by a small flame. At an appropriate time, the priest recounts man's passage through the three previous ages and, following this, a man dressed in a long white robe and wearing a "white star" dramatically enters the kiva but then soon departs. Following this, a rock is thrown into the fire, extinguishing the flames. This symbolizes the traumatic, fiery destruction and the period of darkness that ensued after the previous age came to an end. The congregants then flee from the kiva and are drenched with water in a representation of the deluge. The Hopi say that after their ancestors escaped from the third age, they proceeded to the seven caves and began a seven-staged journey to their present homeland, where they have since awaited the return of their "white brother." In another highly revealing Hopi ritual, a person representing a spirit called Aholi carries a staff to which are attached the figures of seven cornmaidens. During the course of the ceremony, Aholi makes seven stops and on each occasion rotates his staff in a circle.

The Aztecs also told of a series of past ages that were terminated with floods, storms, and upheavals. Since, however, they claimed that "in the beginning" they emerged from seven caves, we can assume that this took place when the previous age ended and the present began. The Aztecs also claim that the land of the previous age was called Atzlan, and the Hopi say that it was situated in the Atlantic.

At a trance session held at the circle of American

medium Jane Roberts, "Seth," Miss Robert's spirit-guide, said to one of the sitters, "In a life in the East, before the time of Christ 1200 B.C., you were a member of a body of men who belonged to an esoteric heritage. You were wanderers and traveled also through Asia Minor.

"You carried with you in your heads messages and laws that had been given to one of your kind in a time nearly forgotten. These were codes of ethics. They had originated from the time of Atlantis. Before that, these codes were given by a race from another star. This race had to do with the origin of Atlantis. The messages were put into words and languages and written down by word of mouth."*[67]

Diodorus wrote that the Atlanteans lived in the land where the gods received their birth and, repeatedly, we have seen that the latter were none other than those known as the Travelers. The Indonesian Torajas told how men were created in "gold" after the appearance of seven mysterious objects. In an Easter Island legend, we are told that the people of the "First Race" were fair and had "shining yellow bodies." These various sources suggest that the Travelers were earth's first people, and it is interesting to note that the Popul Vuh say that the people of the first age were created by god-seven.

The Greeks said that, after the first age ended, some of its people became the guardians of mankind. The Hindus believe that the forty-nine Manus, who came from a more advanced celestial body than earth, were of a race who are mankind's guardians.

Blavatsky explains that the legend of the World Ages suggest that in each case it is the same gods who arrive on earth at the end of each age and help the survivors

*From the book *Seth, Speaks*, by Jane Roberts. © 1972 by Jane Roberts. Published by Prentice-Hall, Inc., Englewood Cliffs, New Jersey, 07632.

create the succeeding era. "At the beginning of every cycle of 4,320,000 years," she says, "the seven (or, as some nations had it, eight) great gods descended to establish the new order of things and give impetus to the new cycle."[68]

African Dogon traditions say that, one day, a "Nommo" will descend to earth accompanied by mankind's ancestors and that a star associated with the eighth ancestor periodically replenishes the earth.

High in the South American Andes, north of Lake Titicaca, is a mysterious, isolated Essene monastery whose order is called "The Brotherhood of the Seven Rays."

Brother Philip, a learned monk who lives there, believes that now is the time for man to open his eyes to the truth, for much sorrow is coming and much of the world's population will perish. After this revitalization, claims the monk, men will come from other parts of the universe to help establish a new civilization.

The first race on this planet, Brother Philip believes, were a tall, well-advanced people called the Els. The Els, he explains, had mastered the ability to travel through time and had originally arrived on earth after colonizing other parts of the universe. They were instructors of mankind's teachers. Some of them had a third psychic eye, and their name is found in the word "Elohim."[69]

The word "Elohim," which is translated from the Bible as God, is a plural Hebrew word and means gods. The Phoenicians told of seven brilliant Elohim, and these are acknowledged by Jewish Cabalists who claim that they travel the universe with seven invisible planets.

Evolutionists and creationalists vie with each other as to the merits of their respective beliefs. When examined from a fresh point of view, however, many world religions show whom they consider the Creator or creators to be. A Quiche-Maya creation legend says "in the beginning"

Gucumatz (one of the seven creator-gods) blessed the arrival of Heart of Heaven (god-seven).

The creation tradition of Zoroastrianism, the religion of ancient Persia, parallels that of the Bible, insofar as it said "seven Amshashpends" created the world in six days and rested on the seventh.

In the ancient Babylonian epic of Gilgamesh, it states "in the beginning" seven gods appeared, while another Babylonian legend, probably written by a woman hater, told how the first women were created by seven evil spirits.

Tibetans believe that the world was created by seven Dhyani Buddhas. The ancient Indian *Rig Veda* says that Visvakarman, the creator, was assisted by seven sages; while Blavatsky relates, in "The Secret Catechism of the Druses," a legend that claims mankind was created after the descent to earth of the sons of God who were linked with seven Mandragoras.[70]

"Marcus, a Pythagorean (and probably a Kabalist)," says Blavatsky, "is said to have told Hippolytus, an early Church father, of a mystical revelation that he had received in which the seven heavens sounded each one vowel and these, all combined together, formed a complete doxology. The sound whereof," adds Blavatsky, "being carried down (from these heavens) to earth, became the creator and parent of all things that be on earth."[71]

The African Masai believe that the Great White God sent to earth Maitumbe, who produced from within himself seven men who were the progenitors of mankind. The African Ashanti assert that God created seven men, who came to earth on a chain, produced men, but subsequently returned to heaven. The Torajoas of Indonesia say that the world was created by Puang Matua, one of the seven mysterious objects within which God traveled.

According to Hermes Trismegistus (an Egyptian sage,

or series of sages), the creation of the world took place in the following manner:

> The heavens appeared in seven circles and gods in their stellar forms being visible with all their signs and the constellations were severally enumerated with the gods in them and the circumference was wrapped around. But the mind, the God being masculine-feminine, originating life and light, begat by word another mind creator who, being God of the fire and spirit, created some seven administrators encompassing in circles the sensible world: and their administration is called "Fate."
>
> The Father of all things begat a man himself who was very beautiful and having the image of his father. [NOTE: The Book of Genesis claims that the Lord said; "Let us make a man in our image."] But, Peomandres says, this is the mystery concealed up to this day. For the nature mingled with the man produced a certain most admirable wonder: for he, having the nature of the harmony of the seven of which I spoke to you of fire and spirit, the nature did not wait, but immediately brought forth the seven men after the nature of the Seven Administrators.[72]

The Greeks believed that the World was created by seven gods, each of whom ruled one of the seven spheres.

In the Great Book of the Mysteries, adds Blavatsky, we are told that "seven Lords created seven men."[73] The Sumerians acknowledged two groups of gods, one of which numbered seven and the other fifty. The first group might well have been the Pleiades, which the Sumerians knew as the seven gods. The second group seem to have been the Anunnaki, or Annage, "The Sons of Anu or An," who will receive our attention at a later stage. The Sumerians believed that the gods were advanced beings whose form was that of man and who supervised the running of the universe. Although no Sumerian creation legend has as yet come to light, it seems quite apparent that the Sumerians acknowledged the same creator-gods as other early peoples.

The African Fon believe that when earth was created, there appeared an enormous serpent that wrapped around it its seven thousand coils. The Hebrews associated the brazen serpent with God, while the Gnostics had a serpent symbol whose head was surmounted by seven vowels representing the seven hierarchies of the septenary or planetory creators.

In the creation story claimed by Churchward to have originated in the lost continent of Mu, we are told of the seven-headed serpent passing through space.[74]

The Battak of Sumatra add that long ago seven eggs enclosing various forms of vegetation once came down to earth accompanied by a magical ring.[75]

Donald A. Mackenzie suggests that the latter was a snake in circular form.

> In primeval times, a maiden,
> Beauteous daughter of the Ether,
> Passed for ages her existence
> In the great expanse of Heaven,
> Seven hundred years she wandered,
> Seven hundred years she labored,
> Ere her first-born was delivered.
> Ere a beauteous duck descending,
> Hasten toward the water-mother.
> Lightly on the knee she settles,
> Finds a nesting place befitting,
> Where to lay her eggs in safety,
> Lays her eggs within, at pleasure,
> Six, the golden eggs she lays them,
> Then a seventh, an egg of iron.

(Taken from the Kalevala—a collection of ancient Finnish folk songs.)

Hindus claim that the god Vishnu traveled on a wondrous bird called Garuda, which emerged from an egg brought forth by Vinata, wife of one of the seven creators.

Some ancient Egyptian sources claimed that the creator was Ptah, an elderly, bearded, white-robed man who was one of the Seven Cabiri and who emerged from an egg.

In *Atlantis and the Seven Stars*, J. Countryman, quoting Professor Humet, draws attention to the association of the Cabiri with the Pleiades.[76]

Chapter Twelve

One evening during the summer of 1980, while I was talking to Gerry and his family, I had the feeling that an outline of a figure had passed close to me but, as I did wish to interrupt the conversation, I said nothing. Gerry confirmed my suspicions, for he said we had with us a spirit entity who had patiently been waiting to speak. Gerry's appearance began to change, and soon we were being addressed by someone who spoke with an American accent, whom I identified as Edgar Cayce.

"That's my name; that's my name," he said to me. "Do you know of me? Well, when I was on earth I used to give many readings to people, and I was able in my own humble way to diagnose conditions that existed within their physical bodies.

"Well, contrary to what others had to say, the country or the continent known as Atlantis existed. It existed. People lived and loved and worked. I have written, and I have spoken to people who lived in this continent of Atlantis.

"You, my brother, have been guided and helped as I was guided and helped. Since I left my physical body and passed into the etheric plane, I have been able to learn much and observe much through the libraries that exist on the etheric plane.

"I would say, perhaps in the next fifty years, contact will be made between the people of your earth and people of a higher galaxy. There has been much talk of this coming together, sharing of knowledge and sharing of wisdom.

"We can assure you that there was definitely a landing of an alien people on this earth. We can assure you that laser beams, machines, and airplanes existed before the time of the floods. We can assure you that the Bible's books start at the beginning, which was really the end of another civilization. We can assure you, my brother, that these people came in peace. They will come again in peace, but they cannot come until this earth plane has stabilized itself. And when they come, they will bring with them the knowledge and the wisdom that their fathers brought to this earth before them."

After our visitor departed, his place was taken by another entity who did not introduce himself but who spoke to us as follows:

"May the power of spirit descend upon you as it descended upon this earth. The power of spirit was the power of the ship. The spirit was the ship and the tumultuous sound was the engine of the ship.

"And the spirit descended to earth and from the spirit came forth the Lord. But no one could set their eyes upon the Lord. And so he sent forth, from the spirit, his deputies, and they looked around them, and they reported to him who dwell in the spirit. And the spirit rose from the earth and there was great turmoil and thunder.

"And the people hid their eyes and they prayed to the Lord: 'Do not strike us down.' And the foolish people ran toward the spirit, and fire came from the spirit and burned them until their bodies were cinder and they said, 'The spirit has sent down the flame from heaven to destroy the people.' But they did not understand that the flame came from the spirit as the spirit descended into the heavens. But, in their own ignorance, they believed that the Lord had sent down the flame from heaven. But no, it was not the fire of heaven but the flames that came from the spirit as it descended into the heavens.

"And the spirit descended into the heavens, and it floated like a star among the sky. Oh, I say to you on this earth, 'Open your eyes to the truth.' Do not be blinded by dogma and superstition. For the spirit descended, taking with it many people. And the prophets descended into the spirit, and the spirit hovered over the earth and it climbed into the heavens."

Our second visitor then departed, and after Gerry came out of trance, we discussed the second visitor's comments and its implications. One thing that puzzled us was his statement that the "spirit had descended into the heavens." Had the word "descended" been used by mistake, or was there some hidden significance?

A possible explanation occurred to me when I was later reading Hopi's version of the legend of the World Ages, which says that after destroying the First and Second Ages, the Creator's nephew (who lived in the eighth world) took many people below the earth's surface. Although this is not mentioned in the story of the third age, myths throughout the Americas and in other parts of the world tell how, after the flood destroyed the previous era, people sheltered beneath the earth's surface.

In ancient Peru, it was said that, after destroying an evil race of giants, Viracocha took some of the survivors beneath the earth, while in Mexico the great white teacher, Votan/Quetzalcoatl, was believed to have traveled through a subterrean tunnel to the "depths of heaven" where he found his relatives "the serpents."

The African Dogon say that before the "eighth Ancestor" departed, he disappeared beneath the earth's surface to a place called the "Ant Hill." The Hopi Indians add that the survivors of the earlier ages took shelter beneath the earth's surface with a people called "The Ant People."

In *Lord of the Flame*, Elizabeth Van Buren writes that the Urgha Mongulalas Indians tell of a long visit to Earth of civilizing star-gods who built thirteen underground linked cities reached from the surface by a long tunnel. As with other American Indians, these people tell of warnings given by the star-gods of mans' delinquent behavior, of a great flood and of people taking shelter beneath the Earth's surface. Elizabeth Van Buren unbeknowingly identifies the star-people, for she says that the plan of the cities reflect that part of the universe from whence these space travelers came and seems to highlight seven important stars.[77]

The Hawaiians believe that a labyrinth leads to the underworld, and the North American Acoma Indians tell of a hole in the north called "Shipap," from which the people once emerged. The Hopi Indians associate the labyrinth with their underground kiva, in the floor of which there is a hole called "Sipapuni," which symbolizes the place of emergence from the previous age.

In addition, the Greek flood story tells that after the flood people emerged from beneath the earth's surface, they repopulated this world. When a new city was consecrated in classical times, the circumbulation of a labyrinth formed part of the ceremonial ritual, for it symbolized a re-enactment of the creation. Many medieval churches show spiral labyrinths on their floors, and numerous mazes were dotted around the countryside.

Earlier in time, drawings of sevenfold, spiralled labyrinths appeared in England, Pompeii, Finland, Siberia, and Knossos in Crete; and maze dances are said to have taken place in caves near Knossos in which a large snake was carried.

The Hopi Indians regard the snake as being man's

elder brother and prominently feature this reptile in their rituals. Hopi labyrinth drawings closely resemble one found on a coin at Knossos in Crete.

The sevenfold spiral was favored by the Etruscans in their art, and special significance was given by them to the "mystical seven." In *Pygmy Kitabu*, Jean Pierre Hallet refers to an Etruscan wine jar decorated with the drawing of a maze, from which a king emerges with his heir and "seven men,"[78] while Peter Kolosimo, in explaining the spiral's connection with the creation, mentions an ancient Japanese spiral drawing that also features seven male figures.[79]

Discovered on the island of Melos in the Aegean was a model of a house with seven circular rooms decorated with a spiral pattern.

In Africa, in the area between the Limpopo and Zambesi rivers, are the remains of the mysterious massive walled settlement called Zimbabwe. When Europeans first arrived at the site, they reported that one of its main structures consisted of a thick, high wall enclosing a secret passageway and a maze of roofless rooms surrounded by seven circular towers.

In the Middle Ages, stories spread through Europe of the exploits of the immortalized hero, King Arthur. In Wales, the bards sang songs of a flood that drowned all of mankind other than Arthur and seven others who survived in a boat. In the ancient Welsh poem, "Spoiling of Annwn," which abounds with the mystical seven, Arthur descends into the underworld to a mysterious place called Caer Sidi, from which seven men emerged. Caer Sidi is suggested to have been a strange revolving castle, and Arthur was associated with the seven stars of Ursa Major.

Chapter Thirteen

When Quatal related to the Sherrick circle the events surrounding the Travelers visit, we were given to understand that it took place in the era of the destruction of a country or continent called Atlantai, which presumably was the lost continent of Atlantis.

As my research proceeded, I discovered certain factors that seemed to pinpoint this era and when I came upon the legends of the World Ages, my suspicions began to seem well founded.

The Mayan Indians recorded that the present age commenced in the year 3113 B.C., after god-seven destroyed the evil people of the previous age with a flood.

Around 3000 B.C., numerous villages sprang up in New York State and, according to Edgar Cayce, the lost tribes entered the southern part of North America and crossed over by boat to Mexico.[80] In Mexico, villages began to appear, and there was a sudden sharp increase in the volume of plants and maize under cultivation. Mexican yarns say that agriculture was taught to the Indians by Quetzalcoatl. The Maya claimed that maize was given to them by the creator-gods.

Ancient Egyptians say it was Osiris who taught them how to cultivate wheat and barley, which had previously grown in a wild state. Osiris can be traced back through the pyramid texts to the era around 3000 B.C., there being no earlier suggestion of his importance.

Ignatius Donnelly writes that the Egyptians placed Osiris at the close of the era of the gods, which he suggests was the time when Atlantis disappeared beneath the seas.[81]

Donald Mackenzie says that the early Egyptians linked Ptah with Osiris and treated them both as one.[82]

"At first," says Lewis Spence in discussing the origin of the Cabiri, "I was under the impression that the myth referred to the entrance of the Azilian peoples to the Mediterranean, but chronological reasons seem to militate against such a presumption, and it appears much more probable that it is connected with a cultural invasion from the west at a much later period, say some 3000 B.C."

"The Cabiri," adds Spence, "are said by Sanchoniathon to have been the inventors of boats, of the arts of hunting and fishing, of building and agriculture. May it not be," he concludes, "that the secret cult connected with the Cabiri emanated from an Atlantis still existing about 3000 B.C."[83]

The era around 3000 B.C. marked the beginning of a new age in Equador in South America, where early signs of civilization appeared; and Japanese Jomon pottery mysteriously appeared on the coast precisely at the time when the Jomon culture began in Japan. In Colombia, South America, the earliest known pottery can also be dated to this time.

Tiahuanaco, the advanced Andean city, was said by Wendell Bennett, to have been at least 5000 years old and, by the local Indians, to have been built by tall white-robed men who had red hair. They fled from the destruction of their former homeland, which had been overcome by the flood.

Around 3000 B.C., settlements appeared on the coast of Peru.

Five thousand years ago, an advanced metal foundry was established in Soviet Armenia and, at Mehrgath in Pakistan, there was suddenly an inexplicable increase in the production of pottery.

The domestication of cattle began in the Indus Valley, as did the commencement of the cultivation of cotton both there and in Peru.

"The story of Mohenjo-Daro," says James Wellard, "begins after 3000 B.C., when a race of people of whom we know nothing but a number of cities, towns and villages in the region of the India subcontinent called the Punjab or Land of the Five Rivers. For want of a more specific term, we refer to this strange and at present unexplained historical phenomenon as the 'Indus Valley Civilization.'"[84]

Of the numerous seals produced by this unknown race, one depicts a "horned deity" in the sky in a vase-shaped vessel, below which are seven men. Although nothing is known of this god, it is interesting to discover that the ancient Peruvians associated Viracocha with a "thunder vase"; and a hymn to Osiris, on the Stele of Sobk-iry, in the Louvre Museum, describes him as having two horns. Osiris was linked with the bull, while Hindu mythology and the ancient Rig Veda tell of Indra, the golden warrior, who was known as "The Bull" and was said to have lived on the sevenfold Mount Meru together with the seven Rishis. Indra, it is said, fought a battle with an evil dragon called Vrtra, which he defeated after sending down a massive thunderbolt. This prehistoric missile broke up mountains and caused a catastrophic flood which completely covered the monster. After this, Indra rescued Manu the mariner on the ark and led him to safety.

In *Secrets of the Lost Races*, Rene Noorbergen says that

The Chinese god of Long Life Shou-hsing. Author's collection. Photo courtesy of Stephen Farra.

Hindu scholars are of the opinion that, in the year 3102 B.C., a nuclear explosion took place on earth.[85] What Noorberrgen omits however, is that the Hindus believe that it was in 3102 B.C. that Manu was rescued from the flood with the seven Rishis and the previous era terminated.

"Polynesian, Red Indian and Siberian tales," says W. Raymond Drake, "tell of several suns burning the earth, which some warrior or animal later destroyed. The Greeks accuse Phaeton of misdriving the sun chariot, scorching whole countries aflame; there is geological and historical evidence to suggest that four or five thousand years ago some cosmic cataclysm did menace our planet."[86]

The script of the Indus Valley people is, in fact, said to resemble that of early China, whose civilization can be traced back to 3000 B.C., when agriculture began.

Although earlier Chinese history is a complete blank, the Book of Y-King says that the Chinese were taught by celestial genii; while Vaughn M. Greene claims that around 3000 B.C., when there were worldwide sightings of white-bearded gods, a man of this description is said to have visited China, educated the people in the ways of agriculture and the arts, and to have given them their calendar.[87]

The Bible tells us Elam was the son of Shem, who was saved with Noah on the ark. Very little is known of the origin of the ancient Elamites, although Elliot Smith believes that they were linked with the early civilizations of China, the Indus Valley, and Sumer.[88] Ur Sumer's first dynasty was said to have been preceded by the flood and to have commenced around 3000 B.C., when cuniform, the earliest known form of writing, made its appearance in the Middle East.

The Sumerians claimed to have been civilized by certain advanced beings, the Annanage, who were led by a council of seven. The Annanage or Annuki, as we have seen, were the sons of An or Anu, who were said to be fifty in number (Goda and his forty-nine assistants?). Anu had seven messengers who traveled through the skies and the depths of the seas; without doubt, these are the gods said by the ancient Egyptians to have emerged from Anu, one of whom was Isis, the wife of Osiris.

In Mesopotamian history, the period from 3100 B.C. to 3000 B.C. is known as the Jemnat Nasr period.

"Almost forgotten since the Samarra period," writes George Roux of this era, "sculpture suddenly re-appears, soon reached a high degree of perfection and, is applied with a passion to a variety of objects."[89]

At this time, in the Middle East, broomcorn millet (which is of unknown origin) made its appearance, and dairy farming began, as did farming with oxen-drawn ploughs. Metalcraft commenced in Eastern Europe, civilization had its beginnings in Greece; while in Crete copper implements came into use instead of stone.

There is evidence to suggest that from 3000 B.C. onwards, men of advanced knowledge arrived in Europe, for along its Atlantic seaboard, huge impressive megalithic structures (and circles) made their appearance; their technical planning is said to have been beyond the capabilities of the earlier peoples. In discussing the significance of the Callanish Stone Circle, on the island of Lewis off Scotland, and of other ancient circles, John Wilcock says that, according to T. C. Lethbridge, they may have been connected with an extraterrestrial visit to earth some five thousand years ago.[90]

Around that time, a huge structure resembling a flying saucer was built at Las Millares in Spain and, so far as the Callanish Circle is concerned, it, like many other ancient structures was aligned to the Pleiades—the seven sisters.

Five thousand years ago, there was built, north of

Dublin, Ireland, a "dazzling white circular" structure known as New Grange. The outside blocking stone is decorated with a spiral. The spiral made an appearance in the area of the Danube some 5000 years ago and from there it is believed to have spread across Europe. In like form, it surfaced in early America and was adopted as a facial decoration by the Maòris. The spiral, as we have noted, has later been associated with the creation or re-creation.

Within the New Grange mound are drawings of concentric circles and a solar barque resembling others on the rocks of ancient Sweden. One rock drawing at Bohuslan and Sutden, in Sweden, shows a boat crewed by a huge "horned or long-eared man" and seven companions, six of whom carry staffs.

Felix R. Paturi says that some five thousand years ago, there was a sudden change in the style of Swedish rock art, which unaccountably became more symbolic.[91] At the same time, hundreds of villages sprung up at the Karelian Isthmus, east of Sweden, just as they were doing in other parts of the world, and rock art in Australia had its earliest beginnings.

In Scotland, around 3000 B.C., a new style of chambered tomb appeared, and Neolithic Stone Age people arrived on the isle of Arran, where one can still see an ancient circle of seven huge standing stones.

In the same era, at Skara Brae in the Orkneys, a megalithic stone age settlement was built whose inhabitants are suggested to have been men of high intelligence. Also at the same time, in the Orkneys, the Stenness Stone Circle and Quoyness cairn appeared, the latter having the form of six outer chambers surrounding a seventh.

In *The Key*, John Philip Cohane [92] suggests that, from a study of world place-names, it seems that there were two major dispersions around the world seemingly linked with the Semitic Middle East, the earliest being on a worldwide basis.

Ignatius Donnelly says that William Penn claimed that the Pennsylvanian Indians so closely resembled Jews in custom and appearance that, dressed in European clothes, they would have passed as being Jewish on the streets of London.[93]

In *Beyond Star Wars*, William F. Dankenbring tells of a discussion he had in Mexico City with Dr. Von Wuthenau, an authority on Mexican figurines.[94] Dankenbring tells us that, from his study of excavated figurines, Dr. Von Wuthenau has come to the conclusion that, at some time in the far past, numerous Semites must have lived in the area around Acapulco in Mexico. In another of his readings, Cayce said that the British West Indies once formed part of the lost continent of Atlantis, part of whose remains would be found in Bimini, in the Bahamas.[95]

Dankenbring says that the Yuchis Indians claimed to have crossed over the sea, from a former lost homeland that was situated in the area of the Bahamas, and to have landed in Florida and Georgia.[96] While not necessarily suggesting that the Yuchis were Jews, it is interesting to discover that they celebrate a festival similar to the Jewish Sukkoth (Tabernacles), use the same name for God as the ancient Hebrews, celebrate a festival similar to Passover and, like many other Indian tribes, have a story on the theme of the biblical Tower of Babel.

The Maori of New Zealand are of a mixed race, some of whom have red hair and white skin. The earlier people of Chatham Islands, off South America and of New Zealand, were the Semitic-looking Moriori who later intermarried with the Maoris. People of this same race live in India, and some of them entered Mesopotamia, Syria, and Egypt around 3000 B.C. from an unknown place of origin. Remains of this people have been discovered near the Great Pyramid in Egypt.

The Phoenicians, the Semitic neighbors of the Israelites who claimed to have been tutored by the seven Cabiri, arrived in the area of Lebanon about 3000 B.C., reputedly from a land devastated by earthquakes. At this time, the early Bronze Age commenced in Sumer and in Palestine. In Palestine, villages suddenly developed into cities, and at Megiddo, seven-staged tombs were built.

In *Technology in the Ancient World,* Henry Hodges says: "The two or three centuries around the year 3000 B.C. appear to have been fairly critical in the history of the development of early technology."[97]

And, in referring to pyramid construction in ancient Egypt, J. H. Breasted adds; "Most of this advance was made during the thirtieth century B.C., that is, between 3000 and 2900 B.C. Such rapid progress in control of mechanical power can be found in no other period of the world's history until the nineteenth century."[98]

American medium Grace Cooke relates that Atlantean wise men came to Egypt and taught its people how to build temples.[99] She also says that, long ago, star men came to the then-existing Atlantis and passed on wisdom and spiritual teaching. These teachings she says, were then spread by Atlantean inititiates who traveled to Egypt and various parts of the globe.

The Great Pyramid, one of the seven wonders of the world, has intrigued scholars for thousands of years, and there are many theories concerning its builders and date of construction. One tradition links the Great Pyramid with the era of the flood. In addition, the renowned Jewish historian, Josephus, claimed that "Sethites," realizing that the world was facing destruction from fire and floods, constructed a remembrance in the form of two pillars, one of which, it is suggested, was Egypt's Great Pyramid.

The white-haired, white-robed spirit guide who took a keen interest in and assisted with this book through Gerry, informed me that much was to be learned from the pyramids, especially from their alignments.

Several of the early Egyptian pyramids have seven levels built into them, and it's not surprising to find that Hindu scholars believe that they symbolized Mount Meru—the seven-tiered home of the gods. In the case of the Great Pyramid, leading off from its sarcpohagus chamber is a shaft aligned to the seven stars of Orion, and the roof of its grand gallery rises in seven levels. Peter Tomkins explains that the unit of measurement used in the Great Pyramid's construction was the septenary royal cubit, which achieved its importance with the unification of Egypt, when it was linked with the Egyptian sevenfold heaven.[100]

In an earlier chapter, it was mentioned, before destroying the city of Atlanta, star men rescued a white-haired man, who it would appear, was known to the Israelites as Noah, and to the Hindus as Manu (the first great teacher and mariner).

In the Middle Ages the seven stars of Ursa Major were described as the home of the "Seven Wise Men" who traveled in the ark with Minos. The Cretans claimed that Minos, father of their civilization, owned a golden staff, sired seven children, gave them their laws, and established their maritime power. Although it is not clear when this remarkable man lived, the Minoan era is believed to have commenced about 3000 B.C., around which time Cretan sea power can be dated and when Egypt was overcome and united by Narmer, whom some believed to be Menes.

Professor H. Thierfelder has drawn attention to the resemblance between the names Minos and Menes.[101] If one replaces the vowels in "Meni" with "a" and "u," we find, once again, the name "Manu." The Egyptian ruler Menes was a remarkable person, for he not only united the two kingdoms, but engaged in major engineering works, altered the course of the Nile, and constructed a huge reservoir.

In *The Illumined Ones*, medium Grace Cooke claims that in her former life she was a Mayan Indian. She tells how her brother, in that life, met a wise man called Menes who showed him a vision of the destruction by fire and water of the peoples of an advanced continent whose ways had turned to evil. Some of the good people, such as Menes, escaped and he became a great leader amongst men. In Isa. 7:14 we are told: "Therefore the Lord himself shall give you a sign; Behold, a virgin shall conceive, and bear a son, and shall call his name Emmanuel." Who then was this great man whose coming was forcast? If we remove "el" from the end of his name, we are presented with Emmanu or Manu, the mariner on the ark and great teacher and leader of mankind.

Polynesians tell of a great man called Maui who was saved from the flood and used his wondrous powers to help mankind. According to Blavatsky, ancient Indian records tell of "Manu Vina" (suggested by her to be Menes) who, together with his followers, traveled from India to Egypt.[102]

Concerning the Narmer Palette, Margaret Murray writes; "One of the most important monuments of the First Dynasty is the slate palette of Narmer. On the obverse, is the king wearing the crown of Upper Egypt. He is represented as being of gigantic size and is in the act of killing an enemy whom he has seized by the hair. The enemy's title is above his head: 'Chief of the Waters.' "[103]

Can it now be a coincidence that the Teutonic peoples

claimed that their first great leader, Mannus, once destroyed a race of giants?

Easter Island, with its seven sacred statues, is renowned for its birdman cult. Drawings of birdmen are not only found on this island but in other parts of the world, including Australia and the Canary Islands; some dated around 3000 B.C. have also been found in eastern Siberia. The Eskimos claimed to have been transported to their new homeland by huge birds. We also note that the Greenlanders claim to have descended from the Eskimos arriving in Greenland some five thousand years ago.

Some 160 years ago, Professor William Buckland conducted a period of research into a probable past world flood. In his published findings, Buckland reported that the state of various animal remains suggested that there had been a sudden catastrophe on earth and that it occurred between five and six thousand years ago.

In a paper dealing with the submergence of the West European and Mediterranean coasts, read before the Royal Society of London, Professor John Prestwich reported that:

The Rock of Gibraltar rose to close the strait, then sank down partway; the coast of England, and even hills 1,000 feet high, were submerged; the island of Sicily was inundated, as were elevations in the interior of France. Everywhere the evidence bespeaks of a catastrophe that occurred in not-too-remote times and engulfed an area of at least continental dimensions. Great avalanches of water loaded with stones were hurled on the land, shattering massifs and searching out the fissures among the rocks, and rushed through them breaking and smashing every animal in their way.

"Prestwich suspected," says I. Velikovsky, "that the area involved must have been much larger than that discussed in his works. He gave no reason for such submergence and emergence. The catastrophe occurred when England was entering the age of polished stone or possibly when the centers of ancient civilization were in the Bronze Age."[104]

In 1949 Professor M. Ewing explored the mid-Atlantic Ridge and, as Velikovsky explains: "the results of the expedition of the summer of 1949 strongly indicate that at some time not so long ago, in numerous places where the Atlantic Ocean is today, there was land and beaches and, in revolutions on a great scale, land became sea thousands of fathoms deep."[105]

In *Early Man and the Ocean*, Thor Heyerdahl points out that about 3000 B.C., not only did civilization take a step forward, but at the same time there appears to have been a tremendous upheaval in the Atlantic, causing Iceland to split.[106] The Helgafell Volcano erupted on the Icelandic island of Heimey with such a force that the island's appearance changed completely. The sea levels along various parts of the coasts of England and France appear to have risen at this time, causing flooding; and people as far away as Crete and Cyprus fled from their homes and took shelter in caves.

At Bimini, in the Bahamas, what appear to have been huge walls have been discovered in the shallow water off the coast, and there has been reported the sighting of a enormous pyramid beneath the seas some fifty miles out from Florida.

"RUSSIANS FIND ATLANTIS" says *London Daily Telegraph*.

Russian scientists have photographed what they believe to be the remains of the fabled city of Atlantis. Dr. Andrei Akesenov, deputy director of the Soviet Academy's Institute of Oceanography said, "Analysis of eight photographs taken deep in the Atlantic showed what appeared to be the remains of giant stairways and walls."

Speaking to journalists aboard the Soviet survey ship *Vitiaz*, moored in the Tagus River at Lisbon, he said that they had discovered what appeared to be man-made structures near a submarine mountain midway between Portugal and Madeira.

VEGETATION COVER

Dr. Askenov said the photographs would be published soon but all the structures were heavily eroded and in places destroyed by submarine vegetation. "More observations and tests would have to be conducted before definite scientific conclusions could be drawn," he said.[107]

Chapter Fourteen

It was the evening of the 24 September 1980, when two other friends and I were invited to visit Gerry at his home. We were discussing trance-mediumship and the paranormal. Suddenly, a gust of cold air suggested that an unknown presence had joined us. I turned quickly to Gerry and noticed that his features were changing and that he was going into trance.

Through Gerry, we were shortly to be greeted by a quietly spoken spirit-guide who told us that, during his physical life, he lived in Moscow. He said that, since being in the spirit world, he had met people from other parts of the universe, one of whom was with him. He explained that he had learned in the spirit world that there had been numerous visits to earth from other parts of the universe.

"This planet," he said, "is under constant surveillance and they would have no difficulty in destroying it if they so desired.

"What I am going to tell you now," said our visitor, "I would like you to mention in your book, for it is important that it be known: The governments of the USA, USSR, and the U.K." he explained, "are well aware that life exists in other parts of the universe, but they have decided not to make the information available to the public. Emissaries were sent to the American government with the intention of arranging a conference at a mutually acceptable venue but this offer was declined."

After our visitor left Gerry's body, his companion took over and tried to speak but, either through lack of knowledge of English or because he was unable to master the art of speaking through a medium, he was unable to make himself understood.

When Gerry came out of trance, I asked whether he had received any impression of the second entity. Unfortunately, all he could tell me was that he was extremely far-sighted and had exceptionally long arms.

Within a week or so of this interesting event, one of the mediums of the Sherrick circle gave me a periodical news sheet concerning UFOs, and this led me to Rex Dutta's book *Reality of Occult/Yoga/Meditation/Flying Saucers*,[108,109] in which I read that it has been claimed, but officially denied, that in April 1954, five flying saucers landed at Edwards Air Force Base in America for forty-eight hours of consultation with the American government, during which time the base is said to have been closed to all unauthorized personnel, while the craft were examined by high ranking officials. Rex Dutta writes:

23rd September 1947, Air Technical Intelligence Center of the U.S. Air Force (the vital nerve center link) wrote officially to the president regarding UFOs, "the reported phenomena are real."

Twenty-nine years later these were identical words used by the French Minister of Defense when France became the ninth government to publicly acknowledge the reality of Saucers.

1949—Telecommunications Special Project of the Canadian Government endorsed the American 1947 report and added that the superior alien science could be understood only by the philosophical approach.

1952—Washington, D.C., was overflown by fleets of saucers for three consecutive nights; U.S. jet fighters often obtaining visual-cum-radar "lock-ons" simultaneously supported by ground visual-cum-radar "lock-ons," only to have them broken as saucers outmaneuvred them.

1952—The British RAF officially (but secretly), recognized the reality of UFO's after the multiple contracts/photos/radar/film verifications during the Nato exercise "Mainbrace."

In the February 1976 edition of *Flying Saucer Review*, it was reported that a top American official had admitted that Earth was being visited by extraterrestials, who were attempting to adapt to our atmosphere.

The article further claimed that in 1951, hundreds of people witnessed a sighting of three UFOs hovering above Mexico City Airport and that, although many photographs were taken, none were made public. The report says that later that year, an American official disclosed that saucers were flown by peaceful extraterrestials who were trying to establish friendly contacts. The same official is said to have stated that the U.S. Air Force had been instructed not to take hostile action against these visitors, whose presence had not been publicized by the Administration, and that contact had been made with the star people, who had made three unsuccessful attempts at landing.

Numerous books have been written about UFOs and closely observed visitations. Many authors, denouncing government cover-ups, have quoted unofficial United States sources as admitting that Earth is being visited by peaceful extraterrestials. Reported UFO sightings by astronauts and unpublished moon mission photographs are also said to confirm the presence of extraterrestials on the moon. Suggested reasons for the official silence are the prevention of panic and the need to keep peoples' minds focused on the threat from the East. Another likely explanation is the fear of adverse effects on religion.

We have seen, in *Genesis Seven*, how an extraterrestial visit to Earth, five thousand years ago, affected religious traditions and customs in all parts of the world. We have found that groups of seven stars have been widely revered, that seven circles have featured in world religions and that, since that distant time, stories have been told of the adventures of groups of seven men. We have also found that religious teachers introduced the number seven into their writings and into the rituals of their followers affecting all aspects of life.

We still follow the custom of highlighting the number seven and, like our distant ancestors, relate stories involving seven men. We also tell of the seven seas, wonders of the world, ages of man, et cetera, and introduce this number into placenames and the names of our commercial products. However, in spite of our religious traditions being enormously effected by the visit of the star men, there is nothing that we have considered that disproves the existence of the supreme spirit whom we call God.

Although having various thoughts as to its nature, the majority of mankind, throughout the ages, has believed in an afterlife. So far as Spiritualists are concerned, life is continuous and we take on a physical form to enable us to eliminate flaws in our character that are preventing our spiritual advancement. Suffering is part of our lesson and wrong deeds in this life may have to be worked out of our system in a later one.

Spirit guides explain that associated with our physical world is another dimension, that we call the spirit world, and that spirit entities often try to influence life on Earth. I, for example, could not have written this book without the initial information provided by spirit communications through Gerry Sherrick. Spirit guides also say that life exists in other parts of the universe on physical worlds that have their own spiritual dimensions. They also refer to the Great White Spirit who would appear to be the divinity worshipped by much of mankind.

References

1. M. Oldfield Howey, *The Horse in Myth and Magic*, 7–11, 116.
2. H.P. Blavatsky, *The Secret Doctrine: Book 1*, 459–460.
3. Charles Berlitz, *Mysteries from Forgotten Worlds*, 152.
4. Rene Noorbergen, *Secrets of the Lost Races*, 108.
5. H.P. Blavatsky, *The Secret Doctrine: Book 2*, 453.
6. *Larousse Mythology*, 76.
7. R.H. Charles, trans., *The Book of Enoch*, 115.
8. Hayyim Schauss, *The Jewish Festivals, History & Observance*, 137.
9. Norval Morrisseau, *Legends of My People, the Great Ojibway*, 60.
10. H. P. Blavatsky, *The Secret Doctrine: Book 2*, 312.
11. Abram Kanof, *Jewish Ceremonial Art and Religious Observance*, 37.
12. James Churchward, *The Lost Continent of Mu*, 23.
13. Raphael Girard, *Esoterisism of the Popul Vuh*, 89.
14. Edgar Evans Cayce, *Edgar Cayce on Atlantis*, 144.
15. H. P. Blavatsky, *The Secret Doctrine: Book 2*, 35.
16. H. P. Blavatsky, *The Secret Doctrine: Book 1*, 437.
17. Elizabeth Van Buren, *Lord of the Flame*, 51.
18. Edmond Bordeaux Szekeley, trans., *The Gospel of the Essenes*, 98.
19. M. Oldfield Howey, *The Horse in Myth and Magic*, 9.
20. Daniel G. Brinton, *Myths of the Americas*, 243–244.
21. H. P. Blavatsky, *The Secret Doctrine: Book 2*, 35
22. Joseph Campbell, *The Masks of God: Primitive Mythology*, 458.
23. Miguel Covarrubias, *Mexico South the Isthmus of Tehuantepec*, 114.
24. Gerald S. Hawkins, *Beyond Stonehedge*, 187.
25. H. P. Blavatsky, *The Secret Doctrine: Book 1*, 574.
26. Austin Henry Layard, *Ninevah and its Remains: Book 2*, 447.
27. Tony Morrison, *Pathways to the Gods*, 36.
28. J. Countryman, *Atlantis and the Seven Stars*, 134.
29. Dr. David Zink, *The Stones of Atlantis*, 8.
30. Dr. David Zink, *The Stones of Atlantis*, 115–118.
31. Donald A. Mackenzie, *Myths of Babylonia and Assyria*, 300–301.
32. Karl W. Luckert, *Olmec Religion*, 37.

33. Ivar Lissner, *Man, God and Magic*, 266.
34. William R. Fix, *Star Maps*, 44.
35. Lewis Spence, *The History and Origins of Druidism*, 85.
36. Donald A. Mackenzie, *Myths of Pre-Columbian America*, 246.
37. W. Raymond Drake, *Gods and Spacemen in the Ancient East*, 76.
38. Robert K. G. Temple, *The Sirius Mystery*, 209.
39. Richard Hinckley Allen, *Star Names: Their Lore and Meaning*, 400.
40. Vaughn M. Greene, *Astronauts of Ancient Japan*, 46.
41. H. P. Blavatsky, *The Secret Doctrine: Book 2*, 2.
42. T. C. Lethbridge, *A Step in the Dark*, 18.
43. Donald A. Mackenzie, *Myths of Babylonia and Assyria*, 300.
44. Richard Hinckley Allen, *Star Names Their Lore and Meaning*, 425.
45. Marcel F. Homet, *Sons of the Sun*, 186–197.
46. H. P. Blavatsky, *The Secret Doctrine: Book 2*, 628.
47. Colonel P. H. Fawcett, *Exploration Fawcett*, 13–14.
48. James Churchward, *The Lost Continent of Mu*, 84.
49. Gualberto Zapata Alonzo, *An Overview of the Mayan World*, 59–60.
50. Colonel P. H. Fawcett, *Exploration Fawcett*, 227, 242–245.
51. Huge Cochrane, *Gateway to Oblivion*, 59.
52. Donald A. Mackenzie, *Egyptian Myth and Legend*, 177.
53. Brad Steiger, *Atlantis Rising*, 55.
54. Thor Heyerdahl, *Early Man and the Ocean*, 284–287.
55. Constance Irwin, *Fair Gods and Stone Faces*, 310.
56. H. P. Blavatsky, *The Secret Doctrine: Book 2*, 790.
57. Harold T. Wilkins, *Secret Cities of Old South America*, 238.
58. Colonel P. H. Fawcett, *Exploration Fawcett*, 83.
59. Donald A. Mackenzie, *Egyptian Myth and Legend*, 177. *Indian Myth and Legend*, 208.
60. H. P. Blavatsky, The *Secret Doctrine: Book 2*, 752–753.
61. Harold T. Wilkins, *Mysteries of Ancient South America*, 29, 33.
62. H. P. Blavatsky, *The Secret Doctrine: Book 2*, 774.
63 Thor Heyerdahl, *Early Man and the Ocean*, 113.
64. W. Raymond Drake, *Gods and Spacemen in the Ancient East*, 219.
65. Robin Collyns, *Prehistoric Germ Warfare*, 131.
66. H. P. Blavatsky, *The Secret Doctrine: Book 2*, 704.
67. Jane Roberts, *Seth Speaks*, 482.
68. H. P. Blavatsky, *The Secret Doctrine: Book 1*, 434.
69. Brother Philip, *Secret of the Andes*, 17–19, 27.
70. H. P. Blavatsky, *The Secret Doctrine: Book 2*, 27.
71. Ibid, 563.
72. John D. Chambers, trans., *The Divine Pymander and Other Writings of Hermes Trismegistus*, 8, 26.
73. H. P. Blavatsky, *The Secret Doctrine: Book 2*, 212.
74. James Churchward, *The Lost Continent of Mu*, 21–27.
75. Donald A. Mackenzie, *Myths from Melansia and Indonesia*, 310.

76. J. Countryman, *Atlantis and the Seven Stars*, 27.
77. Elizabeth Van Buren, *Lord of the Flame*, 81–82.
78. Jean-Pierre Hallet with Alex Pelle, *Pygmy Kitabu*, 194.
79. Peter Kolosimo, *Not of this World*, 101.
80. *Edgar Cayce Readings*, 3.
81. Ignatius Donnelly, *Atlantis the Antediluvian World*, 466.
82. Donald A. Mackenzie, *Egyptian Myth and Legend*, 367.
83. Lewis Spence, *The History of Atlantis*, 211.
84. James Wellard, *The Search for Lost Cities*, 67.
85. Rene Noorbergen, *Secrets of the Lost Races*, 122.
86. W. Raymond Drake, *Gods and Spacemen in the Ancient East*, 82.
87. Vaughn M. Greene, *Astronauts of Ancient Japan*, 119.
88. G. H. Elliot Smith, *Human History*, 382.
89. Georges Roux, *Ancient Iraq*, 82.
90. John Wilcock, *A Guide to Occult Britain*, 275.
91. Felix R. Paturi, *Prehistoric Heritage*, 68.
92. John Philip Cohane, *The Key*, 19–22.
93. Ignatius Donnelly, *Atlantis the Antediluvian World*, 185.
94. William F. Dankenbring, *Beyond Star Wars*, 90–91.
95. Dr. David Zink, *The Stones of Atlantis*, 8.
96. William F. Dankenbring, *Beyond Star Wars*, 86.
97. Henry Hodges, *Technology in the Ancient World*, 78.
98. J. H. Breasted, *Ancient Times: A History of the Early World*, 52.
99. Grace Cooke, *The Illumined Ones*, 39–42.
100. Peter Tomkins, *Secrets of the Great Pyramid*, 321.
101. Hans Georg Wunderlich, *The Secret of Crete*, 166.
102. H. P. Blavatsky, *Isis Unveiled: Book 1*, 627.
103. Margaret A. Murray, *The Splendour that was Egypt*, 13.
104. I. Velikovsky, *Earth in Upheaval*, 50.
105. Ibid, 91–92.
106. Thor Heyerdahl, *Early Man and the Ocean*, 327.
107. *London Daily Telegraph*, 1980.
108. Rex Dutta, *Reality of Occult/Yoga/Meditation/Flying Saucers*, 109.
109. *Viewpoint Aquarius*, July/August 1986 edition.

Bibliography

"Ainu, The." *National Geographic Magazine*, February 1977.
Allen, Richard Hinckley. *Star Names, their Lore and Meaning.* New York: Dover Publications, Inc., 1963.
Alonzo, Prof. Gualberto Zapata. *An Overview of the Mayan World.* Merida, Mexico, 1980.
Annals of the Cakichiquels and the Title of the Lords of Totonicapan, The. English version by Delia Goetz. University of Oklahoma Press.
Ashe, Geoffrey. *The Ancient Wisdom.* London: Macmillan Ltd., 1977.
Atmore, Anthony and Stacy, Gillian. *Black Kingdoms, Black Peoples.* London: Orbis Publishing, 1979.
Bailey, James. *The God Kings and the Titans.* London: Hodder & Stoughton, Ltd., 1973.
Bankes, Georges. *Peru Before Pizarro.* Oxford: Phaidon Press Ltd., 1977.
Barber, Chris. *Mysterious Wales.* David & Charles Holdings Ltd., 1982.
Berlitz, Charles. *Mysteries from Forgotten Worlds.* London: Souvenir Press Ltd., 1972.
———. *Mystery of Atlantis.* London: Souvenir Press Ltd., 1969.
Blavatsky, H. P. *Isis Unveiled.* London: The Theosophical Publishing Company Ltd., 1888.

Braghine, Col. A. *The Shadow of Atlantis*. Wellingborough, England: Aquarian Press Ltd., 1940.
Brandon, S. G. F. *Creation Legends of the Ancient Near East*. London: Hodder & Stoughton Ltd., 1963.
Bratton, F. Gladstone. *The Heretic Pharoah*. London: Robert Hale Ltd., 1962.
Bray, Warwick. "The Gold of Eldorado." *Times Newspapers Ltd.*, 1978.
Breasted, James Henry. *Ancient Times*. Boston: Ginn & Company, 1916.
Brinton, Daniel G. *Myths of the Americas*. New York: Multimedia Publishing Corporation, 1976.
Budge, E. A. Wallis. *Book of the Dead*. Secaucus: University Books, Inc., 1960.
———. *Egyptian Magic*. London: Routledge & Kegan Paul Ltd., 1899.
Bushnell, G. H. S. *The First Americans*. London: Thames & Hudson Ltd., 1968.
Campbell, Joseph. *The Masks of God: Primitive Mythology*. New York: Viking Press, Inc., 1970.
Catlin, George. *Letters and Notes on the Manners, Customs, and Conditions of North American Indians*. New York: Dover Publications, 1973.
Charroux, Robert. *The Mysterious Unknown*. London: Neville Spearman Ltd., 1972.
Churchward, James. *The Lost Continent of Mu*. London: Neville Spearman Ltd., 1959.
Cirlot. *Dictionary of Symbols*. London: Routledge & Kegan Paul Ltd., 1972.
Clark, R. T. Rundle. *Myth and Symbol in Ancient Egypt*. London: Thames & Hudson Ltd., 1959.
Cochrane, Huge. *Gateway to Oblivion*. London: W. H. Allen & Company, Ltd.; New York: Doubleday & Company Inc., 1981.

Coe, Richard. *The Maya.* London: Thames & Hudson Ltd., 1966.

Coffey, George. *New Grange.* Dorset, England: The Dolphin Press, 1912.

Cohane, John Philip. *The Key.* London: Turnstone Books, 1973.

Collyns, Robin. *Did Spacemen Colonise the Earth?* London: Pelham Books, 1974.

———. *Prehistoric Germ Warfare,* 1980.

Colum, Padric. *Myths of the World.* London: Macmillan Publishers Ltd. 1930.

Cooke, Grace. *The Illumined Ones.* Hampshire, England: The White Eagle Publishing Trust, 1966.

Cottrell, Leonard. *The Bull of Minos.* London: Pan Books Ltd., 1955.

Countryman, J. *Atlantis and the Seven Stars.* London: Robert Hale Ltd., 1979.

Covarrubias, Miguel. *Mexico South the Isthmus of Tehuantepec.* London: Cassell & Company Ltd.

Crow, W. B. *The Arcana of Symbolism.* London: Aquarian Press, 1970.

Czaja, Michael. *Gods of Myth and Stone.* New York: John Weatherill Inc., 1974.

Dankenbring, William F. *Beyond Star Wars.* Wheaton, Illinois: Tyndale House Publishers Inc., 1979.

Davidson, Gustav. *A Dictionary of Angels.* London: Collier Macmillan, 1967.

Deeta, James J. F., Anthony D. Fisher, and Roger C. Owen. *The North American Indians.* New York: Macmillan Publishing Inc.

Diaz-Bolio, Jose. *Guide to the Ruins of Chichen Itza.* Merida: Area Maya, 1971.

———. *Instructive Guide to the Ruins of Uxmal.* Merida: Area Maya, 1971.

Donnelly, Ignatius. *Atlantis the Antediluvian World.* London: Harper Brothers, 1882.

Drake, W. Raymond. *Gods and Spacemen in the Ancient East.* London: Neville Spearman Ltd., 1968.

———. *Gods and Spacemen in the Ancient West.* London: Sphere Books.

Dubois and Beauchamp. *Hindu Manners, Customs and Ceremonies.* Oxford, England: Clarendon Press, 1906.

Duckworth, Gerald. *Myth, Legend, and Custom in the Old Testament.* London.

Dutta, Rex. *Reality of Occult/Yoga/Meditation/Flying Saucers.* London: Pelham Books, 1974.

Dyer, James. *The Penguin Guide to Prehistoric England and Wales.* Penguin Books Ltd., 1982.

Eliade, Mircea. *Shamanism.* Princeton, New Jersey: Princeton University Press, 1964.

Elworthy, F. T. *The Evil Eye.* London: John Murray, 1895.

Embree, Edwin R. *Indians of the Americas.* Boston: Houghton Mifflin, 1939.

Evans, Edgar. *Edgar Cayce on Atlantis.* Virginia: Association for Research and Enlightenment, 1968.

Eyre, Ronald. *The Long Search.* London: B.B.C. Publications, 1979.

Fawcett, Col. P. H. *Exploration Fawcett.* London: Hutchinson Publishing, 1953.

Fire, John (Lame Deer) and Richard Erdoes. *Lame Deer, Sioux Medicine Man.* London: Quartet Books, Ltd., 1980.

Fix, Wm. R. *Star Maps.* London: Octopus Books Ltd., 1979.

Flying Saucer Review. West Malling, Kent, England, February 1976.

Frazer, J. G. *The Golden Bough.* London: Macmillan and Company Ltd., 1929.

Giraud, Raphael. *Esotericism of the Popul Vuh.* Pasadena California: Theosophical University Press, 1979.

Greene, Vaughn M. *Astronauts of Ancient Japan*. Millbrae, California: Merlin Engine Works, 1978.

Hall, Manley P. *Old Testament Wisdom*. Los Angeles, California: The Theosophical Research Society Inc., 1957.

Hallet, Jean Pierre and Alex Pelle. *Pygmy Kitabu*. New York: Random House Inc., 1973.

Hansen, L. Taylor. *He Walked the Americas*. London: Neville Spearman Ltd., 1963.

Hastings, James ed. *Encyclopedia of Religion and Ethics*. London: T & T Clark; New York: Charles Scribner's Sons; 1909.

Hawkins, Gerald S. *Beyond Stonehenge*. London: Hutchinson & Co, Ltd., 1973.

Heyerdahl, Thor. *Aku Aku*. London: George Allen Unwin Ltd.; Illinois: Rand McNally Co.: 1960.

———. *American Indians in the Pacific*. London: George Allen & Unwin Ltd., 1952.

———. *Early Man and the Ocean*. London: George Allen & Unwin Ltd., 1978.

"Indus Valley Civilization." *Scientific American*. August 1980.

Hibben, Frank. *Treasures in the Dust*. Macmillan Publishers. Ltd.

Hodges, Henry. *Technology in the Ancient World*. Penguin Books Ltd., 1970.

Homet, Marcel F. *On the Trail of the Sun Gods*. London: Neville Spearman Ltd., 1965.

Hood, Sinclair. *The Home of the Heroes, Aegean Before the Greeks*. London: Thames & Hudson Ltd., 1967.

Howes, Michael. *Amulets*. London: Robert Hale & Company, 1975.

Howey, M. Oldfield. *The Horse in Myth and Magic*. London: William Rider & Son Ltd., 1923.

Irwin, Constance. *Fair Gods and Stone Faces*. London: A.P. Watts Ltd., 1964.
Josephus. *Works of Josephus*. Boston: Harvard University Press.
Kanof, Abraham. *Jewish Ceremonial Art*. New York: Harry N. Abrams.
Kenyon, Kathleen M. *Archaeology in the Holy Land*. London: Ernest Benn Ltd., 1960.
Kolosimo, Peter. *Timeless Earth*. Garnstone Press Ltd., 1973.
Kramer, Samuel Noah. *The Sumerians, Their History, Culture, and Character*. Chicago: University of Chicago Press, 1963.
Larousse Encyclopedia of Prehistoric Art. London: Paul Hamlyn Publishing Group, Ltd., 1957.
Larousse World Mythology. London: Paul Hamlyn Publishing Group Ltd., 1957.
Lehrman, S. R. *The Jewish Festivals*. London: Shapiro Valentine, 1943.
Leslie, Desmond, and George Adamski. *Flying Saucers Have Landed*. London: MacDonald Futura Publishers Ltd.
Lethbridge, T. C. *A Step in the Dark*. London: Routledge & Kegan Paul Ltd., 1967.
Lichtheim, Miriam. *Ancient Egyptian Literature*. volume 1. University of California Press, 1973.
Lissner, Ivar. *The Living Past*. Jonathan Cape Ltd., 1960.
———. *Man, God, and Magic*. Jonathan Cape Ltd., 1980.
Lommel, Andreas. *Masks, Their Meaning and Function*. Atlantis A. G. Zurich, 1970.
Lons, Veronica. *The World's Mythology*. London: Paul Hamlyn Publishing Group Ltd., 1974.
Luckert, Karl W. *Olmec Religion*. University of Oklahoma Press, 1934.
Luxton, Richard, with Pablo Balam. *Mayan Dreamwalk*. London: Rider & Co., 1984.

Mackenzie, Donald A. *Egyptian Myth and Legend*. London: Gresham Publishing Company Ltd.
———. *Indian Myth and Legend*. London: Gresham Publishing Company Ltd.
———. *Myths from Melanesia and Indonesia*. London: Gresham Publishing Company Ltd.
———. *Myths and Traditions of the South Seas*. London: Gresham Publishing Company Ltd.
———. *Myths of Babylonia and Assyria.* London: Gresham Publishing Company Ltd.
———. *Myths of Crete and Pre-Hellenic Europe*. London: Gresham Publishing Company Ltd.
———. *Myths of Pre-Columbian America*. London: Gresham Publishing Company Ltd.
———. *Teutonic Myths and Legends*. London: Gresham Publishing Company Ltd.
Moon, Sheila. *A Magic Dwells*. Middletown, Connecticut: Wesleyen University Press, 1970.
Mooney, Richard E. *Gods of Air and Darkness*. London: The Scientific Book Club, 1976.
Morriseau, Norval. *Legends of My People, the Great Ojibway*. McGraw-Hill Ryerson Ltd., 1965.
Morrison, Tony. *Pathways to the Gods: The Mystery of the Andes Lines*. Michael Russell (Publishing) Ltd., 1978.
Murray, Margaret. *The Splendour That Was Egypt*. Sidgewick & Jackson Ltd., 1973.
Mythology of All Races. Armenian-African. New York: Cooper Square Publishers, Inc., 1964.
Mythology of All Races. Finno-Ungric. New York: Cooper Square Publishers Inc., 1964.
Mythology of All Races. Oceanic. New York: Cooper Square Publishing Inc., 1964.
Negev, Avraham, ed. *Archaeological Encyclopedia of the Holy Land*. Israel: The Jerusalem Publishing House, 1972.

New Larousse Encyclopedia of Mythology. London: Paul Hamlyn Publishing Group Ltd., 1959.

Nicholson, Irene. *Mexican and Central American Mythology*. London: Paul Hamlyn Publishing Group Ltd., 1967.

Noorbergen, Rene. *Secrets of the Lost Races*. London: New English Library, 1978.

Not of This World. London: Souvenir Press Ltd., 1970.

Osbourne, Harold. *South American Mythology*. London: Paul Hamlyn Publishing Group Ltd., 1976.

Oswalt, Wendell H. *This Land Was Theirs*. New York: John Wiley & Sons Inc., 1966.

Otto, Eberhard. *Egyptian Art and the Cult of Osiris and Amon*. London: Thames & Hudson Ltd.

Parrinder, Dr. E. G. *African Mythology*. London: Paul Hamlyn Publishing Group Ltd., 1967.

Pauwels, Louis and Jacques Bergier. *Eternal Man*. London: Souvenir Press Ltd., 1972.

———. *The Morning of the Magicians*. England: Anthony Gibbs & Phillips Ltd., 1963.

Philip, Brother. *Secret of the Andes*. London: Neville Spearman Ltd., 1961.

Poignant, Roslyn. *Oceanic Mythology*. London: Paul Hamlyn Publishing Group Ltd.

Purce, Jill. *The Mysterious Spiral*. London: Thames & Hudson Ltd.; New York: Avon Books, 1974.

Rapoport, Angelo S. *Folk Lore of the Jews*. London: Soncino Press, 1937.

Roberts, Anthony. *Atlantean Tradition in Ancient Britain*. Carmarthen, Wales: Unicorn Bookshop, 1974.

———. *Sowers of Thunder*. London: Rider & Company Ltd., 1978.

Roberts, Jane. *Seth Speaks*. Englewood Cliffs, New Jersey: Prentice Hall Inc., 1972.

Rolleston, T. W. *Myths and Legends of the Celtic Race*. George G. Harrap & Company Ltd., 1916.

Roux, George. *Ancient Iraq.* London: Penguin Books Ltd., 1964.
"Russians Find Atlantis." *The Daily Telegraph.* 1980.
Sacred Circles. Arts Council of Great Britain, 1976.
St. Clair, David. *Pagans, Priests, and Prophets.* Englewood Cliffs, New Jersey: Prentice Hall, 1976.
Schauss, Hayyim. *Jewish Festivals, History, and Observance.* New York: Schocken Books, 1962.
Scholen, Gershon G. *Jewish Mysticism, Merkabah Mysticism and Talmudic Tradition.* The Jewish Theological Seminary of America, 1960.
Schwartz, Jean-Michael. *Secrets of Easter Island.* London: Sphere Books.
Scrutton, Robert. *The Secrets of Lost Atland.* Neville Spearman Ltd., 1978.
Segy, Ladislas. *Masks of Black Africa.* New York: Dover Publications, 1976.
Sejourne, Laurette. *Burning Water.* (English trans.) London: Thames & Hudson Ltd., 1968.
Shanks, Hershel. *Judaism in Stone.* New York: Harper & Row Publishers, 1979.
Smith, G. Elliott. *Human History.* London: Jonathon Cape Ltd., 1930.
Sollberger, Edmond. *The Babylonian Legend of the Flood.* British Museum Publications Ltd., 1962.
Spence, Lewis. *The History and Origin of Druidism.* London: Rider & Company.

———. *The History of Atlantis.* Secaucus, New Jersey: The Citadel Press, 1973.

———. *Myths of Mexico and Peru.* London: George G. Harrup & Company Ltd., 1913.

Spencer, Sidney. *Mysticism in World Religion.* England: Penguin Books, 1963.
Sproul, Barbara C. *Primal Myths.* London: Rider & Company, 1979.

Steiger, Brad. *Atlantis Rising*. London: Sphere Books Ltd., 1977.

———. *Worlds Before Our Own*. London: W.H. Allen & Company Ltd., 1977.

Stewart, Basil. *The Mystery of the Great Pyramid*. London: George Routledge & Sons Ltd., 1929.

Szekely, E. B. *Gospel of the Essenes*. Saffron Walden, Essex, England: C. W. Daniels & Company Ltd., 1979.

Temple, Robert K. G. *The Sirius Mystery*. London: Sidgewick & Jackson Ltd., 1976.

Tomas, Andrew. *Atlantis from Legend to Discovery*. London: Robert Hale & Company, 1972.

———. *On the Shores of Endless Worlds*. Souvenir Press Ltd., 1974.

Tomkins, Peter. *Secrets of the Great Pyramid*. London: Penguin Books Ltd., 1973.

Trench, Brinsley Le Poer. *Temple of the Stars*. London: Neville Spearman Ltd., 1962.

Trismegistus, Hermes. *The Divine Pymander and Other Writings of Hermes Trismegisti*. John D. Chambers, trans. New York: Samuel Weiser Inc., 1975.

Van Buren, Elizabeth. *Lord of the Flames*. London: Neville Spearman Ltd., 1981.

Varley, Desmond. *Seven, the Number of Creation*. London: G. Bell & Sons Ltd., 1976.

Velikovsky, I. *Earth in Upheaval*. London: Victor Gollancz in association with Sidgewick & Doubleday, 1976.

Von Daniken, Erich. *According to the Evidence*. London: Souvenir Press Ltd., 1977.

———. *The Gold of the Gods*. London: Souvenir Press Ltd., 1973.

———. *In Search of Ancient Gods*. London: Souvenir Press Ltd., 1973.

Von Hagan, Victor Wolfgang. *The Ancient Sun Kingdoms of the Americas*. Granada Publishing Ltd., 1973.

Von Hassler, Gerd. *Lost Survivors of the Deluge*. Hamburg: Berlagsgesellschaft R. Gloss, 1976.

Waters, Frank. *Book of the Hopi*. Viking Press, 1963.

Wellard, James. *The Search for Lost Cities*. London: Constable & Company Ltd., 1980.

Westcott, W. Wynn. *Numbers, Their Occult Power and Mystic Virtues*. London: The Theosophical Publishing House Ltd., 1974.

Wilcock, John. *A Guide to Occult Britain*. London: Sidgewick & Jackson Ltd., 1976.

———. *An Occult Guide to South America*. New York: Laurel Tape and Film Inc., 1976.

Wilkens, Harold T. *Mysteries of Ancient South America*. London: Rider & Company, 1945.

———. *Secret Cities of Old South America*. London: Rider & Company Ltd., 1950.

World Atlas of Mysteries, The. London: Pan Books Ltd.

Wunderlich, Hans George. *The Secret of Crete*. New York: Macmillan Publishing, 1972.

Zink, Dr. David. *The Stones of Atlantis*. London: W. H. Allen & Company, 1978.